Toby Olson

Collected Earlier Poems

Also by Toby Olson

POETRY
The Hawk-Foot Poems, Abraxas Press, Madison, WI, 1969
Maps, Perishable Press, Mount Horeb, WI, 1969
Worms into Nails, Perishable Press, Mount Horeb, WI, 1969
The Brand, Perishable Press, Mount Horeb, WI, 1969
Pig/s Book, Doctor Generosity Press, New York, 1969
Vectors, Albatross Press & Ziggurat / Membrane Press, Milwaukee, WI, 1972
Fishing, Perishable Press, Mt Horeb, WI, 1973
City, Membrane Press, Milwaukee, WI, 1974
The Wrestlers, and other poems, Barlenmir House, New York, 1974
Changing Appearance: Poems 1965–70, Membrane Press, Milwaukee, WI, 1975
Home, Membrane Press, Milwaukee, WI, 1976
Doctor Miriam, Perishable Press, Mt Horeb, WI, 1977
Aesthetics, Membrane Press, Milwaukee, WI, 1978
The Florence Poems, Permanent Press, London, 1978
Still / Quiet, Landlocked Press, Madison, WI, 1979
Birdsongs, Perishable Press. Mt Horeb, WI, 1980
We Are the Fire, New Directions, New York, 1984
Unfinished Building, Coffee House Press, Minneapolis, MN 1993
Human Nature, New Directions, New York, 2000
Darklight, Shearsman Books, Exeter, 2007
Death Sentences, Shearsman Books, Bristol, 2019
Collected Later Poems, Shearsman Books, Bristol, 2024

FICTION
The Life of Jesus: An Apocryphal Novel, New Directions, New York, 1976;
        2nd ed. Green Integer, Los Angeles, 2018
Seaview, New Directions, New York, 1982, 2nd ed. Hawthorne Books,
        Portland, OR, 2006
The Woman Who Escaped from Shame, Random House, New York, 1986
Utah, Simon & Schuster, New York, NY, 1987; 2nd ed. Green Integer,
        Los Angeles, 2003
Dorit in Lesbos, Simon & Schuster, New York, NY, 1990
At Sea, Simon and Schuster, New York, NY, 1993
Write Letter to Billy, Coffee House, Minneapolis, MN, 2000
The Blond Box, FC2, Normal, IL, 2003
The Bitter Half, FC2, Tuscaloosa, AL, 2006
Tampico, University of Texas Press, Austin, TX, 2008
Walking, Occidental Square Press, Seattle, WA, 2019

OTHER
The Other Woman, Shearsman Books, Bristol, 2015 (memoir)
Journey on a Dime, GrandIota, Hastings & Brighton, 2021 (short stories)

Toby Olson

Collected
Earlier Poems

Shearsman Books

First published in the United Kingdom in 2024 by
Shearsman Books Ltd
PO Box 4239
Swindon
SN3 9FN

Shearsman Books Ltd Registered Office
30–31 St. James Place, Mangotsfield, Bristol BS16 9JB
(this address not for correspondence)

ISBN 978-1-84861-922-7

CONTENTS

Maps

Worms into Nails

Poems 1965–1967

Poems 1970

Vectors

The Wrestlers, and other poems

8

Birdsongs

We Are the Fire

For Eddie Pomerantz and Robert Vas Dias

and in memory of Paul Blackburn and Larry Smith:
Lights in the Tunnel.

Say I know where you are
Now you know where I am.
—Paul Blackburn

MAPS

The Old Maps

The old maps were not a cartographer's
dream of accuracy. They
described an exquisite
motion in the sky.
The map-maker's intention was
to gather a semblance of it,
but the flat page warped
the globe to circular representation. Ptolemy
walked mostly with his head up
He did not measure things tactilely.

Later, the earth was circumscribed
on square paper, which you could lay
on the ground to notice
its approximation with the edge.
After the spheres & before
the globe, angels were placed
'At the round earths emagin'd corners'
and blew inward protection
against the old fear
of falling.

In the old maps
figures of gods & men
are often found. Alexander
could be seen in his maps, or at least
Alexander's helmet: in some way giving more
credence to his possessions.

Maps are no longer cluttered
with things they describe, except
when *National Geographic* presents
'Shakespeare's Britain',

but here the figures
are stylized
having dismissed the intensity
of the old map-makers, deciding
their approach was inadequate.

The Globe

Think of the globe as the base
unit of all existence, and you
are driven back
                    to the human form
                    (nous of the tongue
Eyes
            of the young woman/Mexican boy
                                        on the make for

the male tourist. They want
                    to jump out/want
                    holding
squeezed, like a woman's
flanks beneath you/palms
pressing globes
                    in the sweat.

When I speak to your breasts
the discourse
                    is elemental/words stay
                    in the tongue
the message
                    palpable / this
most accurate sense of geography
gives the land to the touch.

Who reaches for the globe finds
it won't give out
secrets easily.
                    The moon I take to my bed
smothers
in the refuse of my chest,
and there is no

        word for it—
so
Send the boy hairless down
             to the dugs of the sea.
All things happening in the sand, there
is the sail (comes over the lip forcing
            horizons back
and back, until
            the ship itself comes.
And then
it is that he forgets
the childish exercise / he stands
still on the Big Globe, and sees
into agitations
of its surface.

The Relief Map

If summer were a green map
spilt from the coming out time
like unto a woman
's breath
       the worst
temptation her own
wilderness—as if death mapped it out
as if death
were in the valleys' shadows
as if mountain tops were the life
of some woman / a balance you
could push on the high part causing
the valleys to rise.

You are then
like the seismograph
like the waves
of the seismograph / like a pink
arrow
       drives to the ventricles
to a judgment.

It is hard to bring things
into scale   Hard
to see the pains/prior
to your going up to it.
The assault
is judged by
the lines.   The scale
deceives, you have
only one chance
but—

That the seismograph shows
all forces radiate from the center of liquid (
through which waves
cannot penetrate,
are refracted.

A place where heat waits
                              (the waves cannot penetrate
Like the object of sonar
                              (gives meaning to the waves
a place where death can
wait for you.

Without reference to the seismograph
we felt movements in the solid rock
surrounding the grotto
a place that was
like a woman
split open / her bowels
lost in the flood
of the blood torrent
below us / the liquid center.

This was not on the map
had occurred after
the fact of composition
or if it were here
was not visible
from aerial observation.

But this was not all of it
I mean, the mechanics
and the fear.
I want to speak of the flowers.

There were roses, dying
and transparent   Columbines
bent toward the center
Bluebells
close to the ground
                    at that altitude.

And the thing was
the flowers had grown from the rock
had been forced through
this very rock.

That accounts
for the movements we felt
who were concerned, and
chucked it off/talked
of Geology
and the power of water— or

Paul
        picked some roses for Sarah
        carefully
as if they grew
out of flesh / and
they were delicate

things like the charms of a woman forced
from a depth we could not measure
because it is the source
of all measurement.

A Trail Map (for Miriam)

I have awaited the speech
Knowing
      (always
        so little between us
of what is
possible that it comes slow
      of necessity, and

because this is the largest map
(and the smallest in the way
a dart is small
tho it drive into the soft meat of the head.

     . I .

am slow &
will
      stumble
as I come to it. The rock
bites too / is also
hazardous
     as
the skin is and the nails
teeth eyes the voice
and the tongue often

One Sharp Branch
Dart
Twig (or) Spear
Love—
      there is a trail also
Straight/ into the heart.

The Road Map (for Eddie)

We are allowed the comfort of the map
                turning
                        southward
Utah/24, the line— straight
through Parowan
               It is
the quickest route to Las Vegas / the SIGN

and the windshield reflects
back/that highway 70, the broken line
soon to be completed
will effect the bypass   Parowan

obliterated.

But to think then of another time, the road
flat level, extends
in all directions. I mean

as if no road at all

& they come without such comfort
into that journey of first tracing, the fact
of movement, being itself the map

                   the mountains

are what contain us.

But the map
is not the territory. The words
that they are spoken
is the only fact, and after

words, being cared for, given the fuel
to continue.

    It all remains

in Parowan / his
arm across the pump, the wave &

a Lincoln passes

with comfort of the map.

A Special Map (For Danny)

I give you this map, hand it to you.
It is that you start from somewhere
        this place)   and remains specifically
        behind you. Not when these mountains fall away
            and is shown on any map,

nor those habits of the street, as certain
corridors you chose. It remains

back there,
        your absence, to be (if it will
        closed only
after many days.

The Mapping of Currents

If the lion could speak
we would not understand him.
                              —Wittgenstein—

They had come finally to water / the currents
it was not surprising
                              the ship's commodity being
elemental, that below the seas movements were similar.

And because even
the map-makers had them: wives, lovers, or
young boys to handle
some basic needs,
it figured.

At one time to make
maps was basic, in its way / to
get food from the sea found
that even the seas moved inward to meet
maps of the land, the nets
or the rivers.

THE RIVER
my grandfather, the Peshtago (1949) came up to the wideness of lakes
Crivitz, Wisconsin at the shore, sits watching the town
feet on the gunnels
head cocked back under the hat / the wash sends ripples out
the line is slack/spun
out from the reel, silent, the creel
empty. No fish rise to the wooden bait
the plunker funks in the weeds near the shore (flies study it— And
up stream a muskie rises
to bull-snort through bony nostrils. My grandfather

doesn't care, can name
every fish, its place, knows them by hand, the dorsal fin geared
to which rock cove—

                    (croppies hang deep in mid-stream
along the bank
bass
rustle the reeds.
                 Touch of the scales / origins and habits.

    There is indeed a vague and comforting idea in the
    background that, after all, in the last analysis, doing
    an action must come down to the making of physical
    movements with parts of the body; but this is about as
    true as that saying something must, in the last analysis,
    come down to making movements of the tongue.
                  —John Austin, After 1956

I have seen pictures of women in various postures
and made good use of them.
Dressed in stockings and garters
with hats on / women
in beds without sheets, those who stand for it
women laying, girls without breasts
old women
          young ones who feared it.

And the flesh moved in the hand ignoring
the man, his part in it, to speak to her / he
moves as the tongue moves
across the teeth in a closed mouth.

(And it was easy
to divide the scene, take
what you want, from it
women only & lonely & silent.

If I had a line   If at the end of it a hook
for the fish leaps from the pond
like the word is jerked from the mouth
is the force of a circle closing / that connection
as the water closes over
as the mouth closes when the word leaves
as the fish was a part of the pond
is vulnerable. You got to have a line
at the end of it
a hook.

To map the land is selective judgment
the road map does not deny
contours. The map is not a whole
or essential
              measurement. The word
is not the thing itself.

But the mappers of currents (assuming the movements of fish
drew basic charts
inductively
through the study of floating objects

(and some of them, the said being distracted
ran, in diverse directions, the which finally
brought them to water. We
have commended to Jesus Christ in his mercy & etc, who were never
heard from or seen again
on this earth)

And so I bring my cat into this
as figure of death in the house
and she is the lion below me
for she can creep
is the huntress

in obscure events, the fish on his way
to the boat / I have
a line on her— at night
movement of claws pressing into
a search for the dug in my groin

or is the face in the picture
the man saying—"I have put on
as the lion his plumage, these garters
and in the ways of ritual, tied
this ribbon around your neck" and if she says—
"You bastard, this
is a business arrangement"
she must say it
at any rate
to him.

Johnny, my grandfather
the Sea moved contrary to what I believed, and
in the watching has made me crazy.

And tho it flows into rivers
it comes too late.

You are dead / gone
as I saw in the picture only
the use of a road map that gets you
thru to the end

and like that woman (a mad cartographer
trapped in the measurements / Johnny
I have been a lousy fisherman.

The Last Map

which hangs in the study
  (the bedroom / which is
the map of Ptolemy— Ptolemy
's/world   (all ice floes & absence
of this place we live on
and off.

who sent
men out in all directions
to find if
the land ended
and where.
         & the land was
         at least the land—
         and would be heard from
         eventually.

What we have said
here in this room
or anywhere:

desire/love/death

is measurement

      that's
what a map is (hope
fully correct.

For Ptolemy
whole continents
      do not exist

are locked in the hands of dead men
in their poor dead minds. That's
the latitude
& the longitude of it.

Let each of us bring a stake
and plant it in the ground.
Let the map
be realized. Let the stake

Bloom.

WORMS INTO NAILS

A Recent Letter to Pat Garrett

Billy had said "don't pull a gun 'less you aim to use it"
                    meaning
                    no pun, or
if he didn't say that / died from it
anyway.

The Old West, it
is this letter to Pat Garrett
received by his son (probably not
                              a cowboy

The question of
homosexuality?
among those rough bastards?

for Billy (he has been thought crazed) had
all the ass he wanted
at gunpoint, a knife
close by the eye, in back alleys
                    or out in the open.
Killed his first man at 12, for messing
up his father's honor, after that
one each year (for similar reasons

                    NOBODY
fucked with Billy The Kid.
          that's the point,
or
that I can think that way,
this summer day (1966
girl on the bus, the skirt shakes up,
she *wants* it, the meat (not talk
like a train robbery, like

Jesse James
        might have
(considering the meat an assertion, hard
barrel of the gun)
                "they *wants* to be taken, they
                    loves it"

but does she?)
The skirt rides higher
the gun
smokes, I

look up: 116th street, Columbia
University of Higher Learning, the gun

wilts

(my stop was 110th   &   cameras
                    back

she rideth on   along the Hudson   sunset

        *   *   *   *

The groin's solution is not
the solution
        for Jesse, his mother, for all
        the James boys being mean and nasty
        only
        a mother's love.

But this letter

to Pat Garrett / lost in the mails 100 years.
Garrett who killed him, an accident

(they were friends
and Garrett's son
out to protect his father's honor
against the postal authorities and the press

and the pioneer women
                              (dust for makeup
tough as the plains
intractable muscle, and weary

of the flesh
the journey
insensitive
              and Billy
died in the smoke house
amid the hanging meat / of accident

but the letter
to open it

              for the distance can   undo you

You & Me

I want to write poems like the rest of you
want the hard line of Donne, Smart's common sense
and the balls of great Blake.

To be crazy like
those loony Indians at the Big Horn
scaring the hell out of Jimmy Stewart
& just keep coming.

On the river I will be
the tug-boat Little Toot
fucking the big ships around
full of rich men
in dinner jackets, first class.

And living in the suburbs unbeknownst
I'll fashion arrows dangerous
to put the eyes of giants out
and never miss.

Your poems will be like that too.
I want to believe all this
don't you?

A Knowledge of Women

I go to the laundromat in pure
pragmatics: no sox or underwear / nothing to be seen in
                                        on occasion.
And that's what it takes to wash it out: old clothes, your fly
expose; everything you have is in the bag.

At first I took a book to read
but they were watching me, pretend
to be so formal in the worst attire.

So now it's soap and bleaches
a kind of
seminar, to learn of such
simplicities before the grave.

I sit down with the women with pins in their hair.
The machines have windows, there goes my sox
my underwear, everything
I am or pretend to be.

We shake out our respective bags, and the women
they talk straight to me.

Hair

Who feels the hair grow
on the head & does not fear the barber,
that man takes the limbs for granted

for him the whole
body process, kinesthetic as well as motor
is no term of awareness, he shaves in the morning
no thought of the cut, or blood
the possibility
of its flowing

but the hair coming down from
the head most often
straight. On the face there are curls near
where you talk like the fiery message
that speaks from the mouth
or the cock's
protective adornment that fixes

the eye. Who does not feel
with his hand the purpose of hair, thinks
like the woman who shaves (
in her crotch
for the beach, wishing
to become more beautiful

) the hair.

A Game

I am the people's Konrad Lorenz
from a window on 7th Avenue
Fabre of the day-time hours

but
that's BULL says my wife
don't stand naked in front'a the windows
the rapists are everywhere
and also our friends might walk by

    (I love those strange inductions.

She means it's the girls in the mini-skirts I think.
Can't *see* me up here I say

but that *is* Bull, it's
simple exhibitionism.

I pretend jealousy in my wife
it's a great diversion
and makes me happy.

A Letter (to Paul in Spain)

let me tell you in these winter months
it is enuf
        to keep your ass warm and out of trouble.

Look at all these delicious girls under wraps / they
duck in the doorways,
trailing their husbands behind them.
Bouncy rumps are under those coats
(and down / you stum-ble.

It seems we are all this year like faggots,
we could rub together
and make a fire. O

keep an eye out for the flu.
It could happen to you.

Four Love Poems

1. *after Plutarch*

Love makes a man acute
tho in the business of selling

what he bought the other day
for more than he paid for it.

Love
after simple economics
is simple.   It hardens

the soft man / it
softens the wallet of the other.

And if a man be a dullard
and timorous,
he shall become a fixed beam.

This is like the magician
changes worms into nails

and builds a house with wood
he has passed through fire.

2. *after Campion*

He builds in his head a garden
of edible things, and things merely
to look at,

and then he goes outside and finds other things
like walls
to put around it

or fences
or a row of strong trees to guard it,
and then he sits and looks at it.

But now after a while it becomes liquid
and flows out around him,
and he seeks to harden it,

and then it becomes located and hard like metal,
slick nuts and cherries
you could break your teeth on,

and he can't get in.
So he tries again to soften it.
He starts all over again.

   "Oh love there are always fences to build
   and these need shoring up
   and occasionally

there is danger." He says this
while trying to soften it. He is like a squatter
raises an homestead, against the cattlemen.

3. after Herrick

He takes her out shopping
and is framing a verse in his head
about taking her shopping
and what it amounts to.

Then she takes up a garment
and he writes it down
and revises it
and she puts it down.

But her shoulders he finds are like breasts
rounded and covered with natural fabric.
When she moves he moves also,
is the trail of a garment behind her.

And so he takes her home
and makes love to her.
Where he touches her skin like rich fabric,
he pretends he could set it in order.

4. *after Donne*

Now he finds he has spent his time
running around crazy
in the head

and not the least of it, chewing
on bark
and learning all the names for all the trees,

and strange things would happen
and people would look at him
thinking him strange.

But then he discovered the same thing
was happening in her head,
the same running around, chewing and naming.

Now love, we have put the backs of our heads together
searching on maps
of latitudes and sea-discoveries.

O   Circle   Circle
let us rotate in
closing the year around us,

let us come eye to eye. Where
can we find two better hemispheres
under all the friendly planets?

Making Faces

I am always making faces: at people
at animals, a dog's face

and asking the mirror about
the fairest one of all, I get a face
with a bark in it. Often

there are faces in private
(hair of the dog
         which is also lovable)
         me / bearing a child
         I walk like a duck or
                     other animal.

But rare are the faces
hard earned, made for my friends
returned with the same simplicity.

O Mirror Mirror on the wall
the work is
to find your own face
         & make it.

Spring Song

Spring is here
and on the side-walks coast to coast

this year / I'll
have nothing to do with it.

Too many people are dying
from other pastoral devices.

This poem's an emetic for
spring's caught in the throat
'Green grow the rashes, O' there's

no de * ny * e * ing

'How can ye chant, ye little birds
an' lea'e us nought but grief an' pain,
                        For promised joy.'

            yet

birds
        /
            sing comes on soft to me
            bends to me
            Spring

can really   hang you up   the most.

Wood Song

"I cannot bring
men unto women or women unto men,
but only
in so far as a song can / I sing
them together.

In a dark wood
Moss, in a dark wood
Sap
suck'd from the dark root."

O Ariel
spirit in the bark
lock'd in the dark limbs

Tit
twit / twit

a bird so
delicate, so various
ly fashioned

you cannot touch it
with your hands.

The War At Home

You look old by getting old
& haggard
or you get fat and lose it
continuously.   That's the second way.

Every time now
I look at the mirror
I see my brother's face, a slack
in the skin looking
back at me.

There is nothing I would die for
would
         compromise even
my brother, should it come to that
question.   It doesn't

because I want to lay it
on him again in the old way
to rush it, criticize and force
the growing up
to go past that age
or (getting old & losing weight)

to lay my chest upon him
in an older way.   But more

because it has become self-
interest.   My brother (

my face, at 21, the ripe blood ready
for draining). My brother and me, we're sweating it.

We have good reasons.

Jesus Sense

What you can leave behind you is not simply given
nor is the new wood taken up without cost.

We must become as little children
whenever that is called for
and ask the wide eyed questions.

But the role of the loving angel does not allow thumb-sucking
nor a hand in the pants for security.
When you carry the wood you carry the splinters also.

For even the most dangerous action can be done childishly,
observe how the-state of the nation
can be called a game.

We must become as the little children
who believe in direct causality
like knives to wounds and other

simple prediction.

Getting It Down

I am now 10 years distance
from the age of my father's death,
and tho he spent 15 years in dying
I am strong of body
and have 5 years on him.

I know a man in San Quentin
who walks between guards to his visitors.
He is accused
of killing 7 people
among them his mother and 3 of his wives.
He has been given the death penalty.

My clearest memory
of my father is his climbing a walnut tree
in El Monte California
because the nuts within reach were diseased,
and there were good ones on the higher limbs.

I remember
his struggling in the lower branches,
the wormed nuts falling around us,
his crutches leaning against the trunk.

When my friend in San Quentin walks between guards
they yell
Dead Man when someone approaches.
Whoever it is
he must run to the side, and turn his head away.

My father was like a dead man for 15 years,
and in the process of his own dying
killed each of us a little.

Seeing my friend in San Quentin
is like seeing a dead man,
tho he has 15 years on my father.

I have a brother in California
who is constantly changing his appearance
and now wears an earring in his left ear.
I have a younger sister with 6 children.

I have a mother who is married to an alcoholic
who requires a lot of care.
I visit a murderer
who is as old as my father would be.

I remember my father in that rotting tree,
going after a few lousy walnuts at the top,
his struggling and the diseased limbs.
I think (given the circumstances)
San Quentin
is as good as any place to die.

Barracuda

his failure
is immaculate

He is Silver

in the sun
on the beach where they lay him down / one
clean. red. gash, behind the gills.

he is masculine.

what old fish eye / what
immaculate silence

serves you, like
the Barracuda dies from a shark bite / his mouth
Opens

then closes upon nothing.

what immaculate failures / what incredible notions

there is death involved

they will hang the Barracuda, anyway
to dry in the sun.

Meditations (for John Coltrane)

1. *Love*

For once say it straight out and not obliquely
Love is a pain and a burden,

but is
the care a woman gives to a man beyond poetry
or music
        (even should he sing
          with great care.)

I said a B u r d e n:
at night the winter air
cut
    /

        through by rain, the impossible
        job for umbrellas and raincoats.

P a i n
of putting even your clothes
and yourself totally
in the care of another's hands.

what can never be said straight out
but only
obliquely through poetry and music

as vague and vulnerable
as the wind is
cut through by this driving rain—

a pain then
and a burden.

2. Consequences

"meditating on this through music,
however, remains the same"

piece of metal

bit between the teeth, air and valves
the same
burden, bruising through music.

and from these acts, a shortness of breath
the indefinite pain
below the diaphragm.

"I want to be the opposite force"
at work in the world
(survived)

Bring him not up out of dust—Alice
his four children—
survived

by the history of music—
the consequences
of his acts.

3. Serenity

It always returns to woman, who is
Goddess
        light-footed and beautiful
        intruder in the world
of men and what they have made of it.

For it is always she who remains after
the dead have been carried away
and stands in the sadness
of our results.

Not by desire of love alone
is she embarrassed and frustrated
but by money and new clothes, by war
and by contrition for what she has given us
and for what we have done with it.

But there is never a man who is sad enough
nor ashamed enough.
And the movement is always the same
going back to her
bringing her things she didn't want.

Yet we always return to our women—
as embarrassed
and frustrated, as we have made them.

POEMS 1965–1967

Envoy

Lady of the bed rocks / breast tucked under
            the coppice
of wings (and
under the wing, this fruit I sing praises of
or sung to them what hears it)
            Bring
not the in-
fluence of words in the shapes of birds
We
that look up only because of
the wedge tears the sky,
leave the one bird
            pass him by.

Lady/ be not the Muse the
invocater
the bringer of structures of passion / be a sister
a woman   a lover   come with
the whole of the body,
your own smell—

bring it in   now .

From a Window

Winter. Sun breaks on the walk, snow
packed to the curbs: the street
revealed as wider. There are children running
around the newstand (corner
      of 86th & 2nd) the blind
newswoman counting out the dollars.

It's Sunday, and
he walketh out St. Francis
from a window made thinner, more ascetic

      and walketh in slush
      (*Times* under his arm)
      a gloved hand known delicate even through
      the glove or mitten.

It is
    the concern
St. Francis you show to the children, the way of your step
tests in the snow—the slush around you

as I sit with a broken foot / three days since it happened
as if an appendage hung delicate end of a leg.

But the children
are flying around you St. Francis, the feet goeth
      and the birds
how they clung to your shoulders / lived in your hair
(how they shat there) the rape of your ears, built
nests in your pockets
and loved you.

And I hate you
St. Francis your going

(he carries the *Times* under his arm) and
what can I read of the world—
       my foot—
and we heard the bone break like a rifle shot, we
cannot hear from this distance: a place
where care of the feet is imperative, life depending
on motion.

It must be explicit:

this war that murders the feet of young men their intention
to carry the body forward, with warm sox, Desinex,
the toes pointed inward, transmitting force to the calves, kills
the eye-sight also
       the eyes of no use but to scream
it is upon them / Pain
at the arch of the step, and
walketh out.

St. Francis, there are 26 bones in each foot
52 required to enact walking, at least
that many articulations, then:
the tendons, ligaments, fascia, the muscle
fatty tissue, the skin of a like movement necessary
to enact walking—the spaces
between them at least 94, multiplied
in movement geometrically.

       And the spikes
       like murderous birds that annihilate motion
       their beaks looking out of the ground

and the spiked logs in the trees giving only
that time to allow that exposure
      Hyoid / bone figure
of no articulation anyway

   repeat it:

tuberosity of the navicular partly obscured by the shadow
head and talons of a great eagle, cuneo-
navicular joint of the death
beak.
Between metatarsal III and the lateral cuneiform bone
the force of the death
beak, joint between metatarsal II and the immediate cuneiform bone
the fossa containing the immediate eye.
joint between metatarsal I and the medial cuneiform bone
the death   beak.

The function of the hand and foot is
very different, the similarity
between them greatly modified
thus: the foot forms
a firm basis of support
for the body in erect posture.

But the hands
(he carries the *Times* under
his arm) the action of which
can be separated
     like
blindness in one eye, we accommodate
in both
     like a ruined foot
is rendered of no further use, permanent
or temporary.

But the eyes are set in the skull, the permanent fossa
at age 3 the sutures
have closed protecting the brain from all
assault in external forces

we cannot feel from a distance.

But my foot
          St. Francis that I feel the blood now
circulating (which is also healing)
and even that is painful.
That the pain is forgotten, being translated
back to its place for the walking
at one with the legs motion.

          He walketh
out and the feet take him
along the street
          his prints in the snow fanning
the shapes of birds.

And it is Sunday: the papers
are sold, the woman gone home to her cages
of birds singing.

That she could kill them. That there is
such power.

That we possess it, taking
pleasure in the flesh always.

That the flesh lives only
when you see it as extension
of yourself.

That you must begin
with something to hate,
and only then
will you love it.

Concerns

When the chicken peruses her eggs the concern is aesthetic, tho
indiscernible to the human eye. The farmer
tho moved by the chicken
has eyes on proportionate weights,
a guide to the packing of flesh. The egg man
confined by the uniform
shape of his crates, reflects categorically
on questions of size.
But O the magnificent duck, un-
believably left / behind in the cause of creative
farming, she is the true intellectual.
Calling each egg
an 'experience', a product at odds with her times,
she awaits her particular
crates.

A Song (for Woody)

Deep in his grave lies Henry D.
Thoreau no ecstasy, his box
of bones embraces all night long.

In a small cafe, the park
across the way, a children's
carousel, a chest.

NUTS/ I

see over these mounds to other hills, that move
as the breast rises—Oh Walden!
you speak-easy of the mind

        there are no places far enough

away over the mountains I want to go, H.D.
Thoreau the sexy valleys

        to the pond, to

believe in
what the book   SAYS

        that there are such places
        that it doesn't end
    &

I'll be seeing you.

For Diane Wakoski

The Trouble with This House

                                 is in the rafters

partly. Dark birds in the eaves. Be-
tween the slats come FROGS all
in their natural colors
green green from
behind me
green. There

is a river is the trouble with this house
and trees
around it & the frogs from all
sides come into it. Green
grass & the trouble is
the yard the yard is not big enough
for the people & the president advises
FROGS in through the slats by the hundreds
I can't help it: first with my tongue
I am reasoning my teeth
with a club I am beating them
killing them . which is
a large part of the trouble is
        HAPPENING
    this is HAPPENING

This is the Trouble with This House.

Disney

My mother told me that it wasn't so, no death in it,
and the ring of fire, always that it would dissolve, come up
the other scene, hoof against hoof
    & nuzzling they turned their backsides to us. The resolution
    comes before the end. Bambi
    goes with his tail up, from the light, back
    and into the dark of the forest.

                        And Dumbo
(next year saving for three weeks, in a can I buried
in the back yard 45¢, 30 to eat, and the rest
for admission), and saw the ears lift
    that tremendous weight
    upward, as the magical crows sang black-faced
    in the slow
    arc of his first curve.
Only later provided the structure
of Pilgrim who carries the heaviest weight
the brown flux of color
of light edging between his groinless legs.

2

When they brought him out
& into
        the light of day, brightness
dissolving what action was going on
before him,
        until
the flat cow appears / takes on
roundness; then: a chicken, a hog, a duck, some horses, & other
animals of various description.

Thomas
what we have we have in the book
or on film & nothing else.
Quote: they being killed before his eyes, the said
Thomas Granger followed
in a similar manner.

3

In *Dumbo* the Negroes had the best parts, they
could sing and dance / fly quick and easily
(being crows) they were nice people, even
they made up a song to commemorate the strange event
and it was clever. Dumbo
not forgetting he is   *literally*
an elephant, is careful
                                where he steps.
Pilgrim was also careful
with Mr. Timorous, Mrs. Diffidence. It

isn't the same.

4

I should have been aware that he
who took my coat on the school grounds
was Mr. Cowardice, in the guise

        of Mr. Greed, but he was big.
        I mean

he *took* it.

Who needs such knowledge? I
needed Thumper
& Flower
&
plotting.

5

& there were places he could fall into
or slide
          in his flatness
down between stones & the whole way
was full of seducers
                    and that made it worse.

Saved
by his lack of balls, he
depended on grace.
                    Thomas,
it was not to confront the world
or to provide
yourself a place in history,

but fucking
just under 30 animals, one after the other
in arbitrary sequence

P i l g r i m ' s   P r o g r e s s

6

I am back to the theatre of action, where
things are obscure.

Bradford tells me one thing
Thumper & Flower
another.

I could not sit with anything
but the book

& if you brought me the coffee
& cornflakes
                what would they taste like? I have
no single question
                of importance,

but to learn how his foot works, the flat message
sent out at a great distance—

to plot out the rescue of Bambi

I would not try
to look around them.

7

In the face of such horror
Thomas
you escaped in the end,
        went
into the forest.

And you were Pilgrim
who left
        his balls behind.
Nobody found you. You were
that thin.

I will put
Pilgrim into heaven
which he deserves
after such a trip.

Dumbo
(with the help of those Negroes)
            is safe
anyway.

But Bambi
the great buck we forget about
who has grown through the passage
having learned
from the hunters a proper fear, who possesses
the equipment necessary
to kill them
                walks through the woods in his histories
                & there is blood on his antlers
                his giant balls swinging
                Faline at his side

who have escaped the ring of fire
and are still
going.

Every Time (for Sara)

I controlled the action of the high-rent district
                              Boardwalk
                                        all the way
thru Penn/sylvan i a, on down
to Pacific Avenue, in short
                              the whole line—minus the right
                    of way of the Short Line.
I mean / *owned* my open roadster, and drove it. Oh
                    the comfort of great wealth.
& in the beginning I would deal
(Who-ha) trade the Reading, then
build tenements
on Baltic in the slums.

                    O Foolish Woman
                    truck along
                    carry a thimble (or domestic iron)
                    no head at all
                    for the figures of business.

But in the end nobody comes. I have
outpriced the market,
                    everyone
visits Illinois or Tennessee
traveling on the railroads, they
don't visit me.

& so one day I take the big car out
to think. Let's see—

general repairs on all my property.
I was assessed for paving.
The payoff, for the chairmanship.

This car is suddenly
                    well beyond my means.

SO
take a chance / ad - vance
to the B & O   and park it.

The rent is
                    WHAT? 400dollars?!

Name o' the game! she says,
that iron in one hand, fist full of cash

& also pay
the poor tax.

A man would do better
had he stood in jail.

THE BRAND

The Brand

The picture is its own reality,
as they say—
        a fixed point in the galaxy
        of recent stars
        spinning,
over us and our own
times.
        two friends of my mother's childhood,
        one now dead by her own hand / the other
        ran away with a black man

        the dog no longer jumps
        quick in the line of dead trees—
        is a Dog Star.

&

in another: hard in the line of dead trees,
the vertical
        (walnut tree)
the horizontal:
white picket fence, chipped paint, of cheap wood,
hard in the line of dead trees & the fact
                    establishes
                    itself:
October, 1946—
standing in blackface for Halloween
I was 9 years old, as
Uncle Tom, the slight
rake of my hat.

Went out
me and the Mexicans

in California, the first black man
seen in my own face.

Year's end. The leaves fall
like bombs to the ground:
Fire.
In those piled leaves
smoke, in the houses in cities,
fire
in a certain season—the leaves
my father raked
around the tree where I danced
in my black face,
my crooked hat.

      Of burning.
      of smoke the sharp sting of the smell
      at the back of the throat, as
      a house burns & the smoke
      comes down from the fire
      & bites at the eyes
      & the throat is choked
      and fire
      burns from the eyes
      that pass in the street

or else are lowered—
passing.

2

Lane was the best basketball player in Bisbee, Arizona.
He was the only Black out of 600 students,

but everybody liked him.
He was *that* good.

The ball
is the moon's orb, it
doesn't sink, but

$$R\ i\ s\ e\ s\dots$$

...

   is a ball of fire.

3

I talk to my wife in smoke—
the beginning of Spring,
she
crosses her legs, settles in.

Smoke
settles around us: cigarettes
the Spring haze
outside people going, with their coats over
their arms. This
is a season of joy
we talk about that.

   Horns on the avenue & voices, &

above us a man spins in the sky,
2 men spinning.
a man stands on the moon,
a soul on ice.

      My wife says
      they should send poets into space

it wouldn't be the Bible they speak from
but
poetic things, not
"God's in his universe" out that porthole, but
"Jesis—look at that!"

the things I'd say.

The legs
uncrossed
are open
slack, the cigarette—
one puff and the taste is gone, a certain
sadness.
Vulnerable

a drunk black man bellows on the sunny street
smoke over us
a man spinning in the sky.

My wife
who has slept with a black man
can speak sadly
a remembrance of fire
between them. I
cannot speak of him.

A man
stands on the moon.

4

And who would have thought the flowers
would grow up again (out of that debris

a season of fire).
                    they come
&the trees too, their leaves
the people
                at walk in Central Park
                these days
pictures
I see in the album, of Spring
of 40 relatives in Easter
dress that changes the face
fire of violets
in that other park in Illinois.

The brand the new leaves make
on their faces
                    a remembrance
a relief so old even in these
dangerous faces / displaces
whatever pain
they could admit.

                I mean
                everything is A-ok.

Oh my incredible relatives
that face I carried out of Illinois
down to the Mexican border,
my forefathers, a white face
that never saw a black face
anywhere, but that he was a sweet man, a kind
of shuffling animal
to be loved bringing coal
or taking
bottles away—

who are blameless: the Western
Electric Company Bulletin,
the belief in pain
as punishment
to be lived as payment
for vague ideas
of salvation.

I am—as they say—the hero of your poem:
a favored nephew, son & brother
your heritage
of crazy Swedes in long boats under the stars
of dancing black faced against the burning of leaves.

A Jew
by marriage, tho
a simpleton in my western speech

        a man
        spinning over us.

        Her legs are slack.

        smoke / spirit
        of a black man alive
        in the body of my wife.

5

A Spring night.

Smoke.

The white face of the moon.

A man standing on the face of the moon.

A needle
driven into the brain.

2 men spinning.

Fire. Andy
who I have never met, spins
in the galaxy of my thoughts,
your dark star
shining
behind her eyes in talk,

a certain beauty
I value

that soft voice
touching
in her skin.

* * * *

He/I is then ourselves the brand, his face
of hard lines, the burnt cork
faces
the smoke in the winds
of change / flames
                    in the burning leaves
                    raking
                    in his mind a man spinning
                    this picture
                    and again
                    smoke

                black faces
                    /
                mirror.

Let him come—as they say—as the world turns
the fixed stars visible
                    in the sky over countries
against these tall buildings, a light
over Harlem
above this smoke.

* * * *

Let me come as a black man
with a white face
                    in a season of fire
                    in a sad country
as out of a picture
as a man without color
who can only try to live
face to face
with you.

POEMS 1968–1969

The House

Politics being the measure of sadness,
I walk sadly down these streets.
Each man being his own history
becomes historical.

The walls of these houses are 14 inches thick,
and behind them, in back yards, clotheslines
running on wooden poles,
and alleys running behind these houses
full of the leavings of spring

        cleanings of attics
        and old garages, that were

(was) a barn behind my grandmother's house
in 1887, her father
built for his building trade
to house the horses,

        she
        ain't gonna leave this house no longer.

History—
a house like this one
walls, 14 inches thick
and made of brick,
a cistern,
a pump for rainwater in the back.

Politics—
being Charles Gerny's name
on the cornerstone of City Hall, Lyons

Illinois. Police station
housed in the same building.
his daughter, my grandmother
getting my tickets fixed,
putting the house up for security:
$10,000 bail, aggravated
assault with intent to kill,
    a fractured skull
    a ruptured kidney.

History, but
politics in the way they built,
saws
into the living wood

they cut down,
the sap still running from,
till the boards were planed,
dried in the sun.
Nails driven
into the barn of breathing wood.

No wonder
they think foolishly of us,
long hair & beards,
our wearing of funny clothes,
that concern
with
    "literature."

Clayton
must have lived in a house in Indiana:
his awkwardness in apartments,
that distance off the ground.
Must also, have smelled the meat on his father's clothes.

And George,
the bread still coming hot
out of Montana, his mother's tough hands,
his father,
still fishing in that river,
dating
the no-trespass signs.

Stone & Mortar
we have in common
against the zodiac
is a kind of politics,
a history
to walk away from
or into.

We have cause to love them, to
consider their hard mythology
dragged out of deep stone quarries—
as they say—
out of the bowels of the earth.

My grandmother
doesn't nod yet, but
gets lost sometimes.
Was
        no bathroom in those days,
        washed
        in a tub in the kitchen
        once a week.

They were Germans,
before we hated them,
with heads like anvils
upon which

the weather did not strike,
was absorbed, hardened
to political resolve.

Snow
on the level even
as deep as the hip. My grandmother
drove her father's team
pulling the skids of lumber
down State Street,
10 years old,
outlived two husbands
and a son.

Ain't gonna leave this house no more.

What we have in common,
we call it
"literature"
even
the crazy alchemist, working
all night over his fire
we take casually
into our poems.

We must
make no mistake about them
(midwestern & mad as they are)
a house does not build itself up,
and there is no romance in it.

 The maze was not built by magic.
 Thor's roots are Germanic.
 The black bull sweats in his fields, he
 is a working bull.

Politics . History
a thumb hit with a hammer.
Venie
taking that trip west in a broken train
with my real grandfather,
my father 6 months old.

My father's father
the only tow-head
in that family group
of faces, the Swede
they say I look like,
dying at 30 from consumption—

today your grandson
brags in the city
should he go on the pavement in winter
scantily dressed.

   There were
   no bulls
   raging in dark forests, no maze.
   Horses, blowing & stomping on straw.

This house, then
   built in the abstract
out of hardwood
and brick, that was
made out of stone and sand,
   dug out of the ground,
as place to live in.
No pride in it
or humility,

but History,
a place to go from,
Origin.

I would give myself back to the land
but this house stands upon it,

      as if by magic,
      is given to me.

I give myself to the house.

Shoes

Passing on widened streets
the workmen gone
still
a busy area:
building, going up to the left,
walkers pause on the new curb.

Pass
that pot-hole, my wife stepped into
twisting her ankle.

    Bad pot-hole
    Bad Con-Edison
    Bad
    administration somewhere
    busy with other things,
of lesser importance.

2 girls
wearing some strange shoes,
very much like oxfords
(being the new style) pass
by me—

    why
    in the hell is he looking into that pot-hole?

don't see
it's their shoes I'm looking at.

    Good shoes.
    paid Good money for them.

Only, the heels are dangerous: too high,
but they're wide enough (set off,
by contrast,
beautiful legs).

I hold
my wife's foot in my hand:
it's swollen and ugly,
the toes like sausages.

She's beautiful tho,
takes it—so to speak
in her stride. Good woman.

An Ace bandage.
My little joke:

      Cute little piggies.
      Cute sausages.

Yr father was right tho:
Oxfords, Oxfords, Oxfords.

Species

Her feet are gorgeous
she goes among people
she washes the food.

She lives in moist wood, her flesh
is gamy and seldom eaten.

When she goes among people she is able
to endear herself.

She dies of old age.

And those stalk her, and L
waits for her.

        And L names her / she is
breast belly & limbs, and

a head on her shoulders and a spine
going away.

And coming
from another direction she is wood song.

Nameless,
she goes among people
who believe in L.

Her death is genocide.

What she is, when
she is here
is here.

Name

Talk of the bright stars in this sky,
and handling them
    bringing them
down over us,

and the birds too
sexy in evening's light.

Tongue
given to them, words in a bag I carry
page of the calendar turning

    in the breeze / yellow bird
    flits in the bush
    before me—

name
is not origin.

Beginning
with *L*, the first word
inversed, the back yard,
then *O*,
    pond of that shape / A
LOad of lumber, brought from the dump.
LOg keeps
the house warm where you sit.

Tuesday,
sun so hot,
felt like a natural man
out on the beach—
it was

that smile
under the crook of your arm.

Wednesday / Loin
                 against Loin.

Rain
under a dark sky today.
4 birds still in the sodden bush.
Log keep the house warm
    where you sit. *V*
    the ducks rising
    off this pond
& forming.

is Voice, is
going to the store.
is coming back again / always
as Vortex, is filling
the Void, is
the sixth sign of the zodiac,
is Variant,
is Volumes written
against it, is being Vaguely
squeezed in the jeweled Vise.

E is for everything else.

Name is Love.

The Jewry

if it's not one thing
it's another
           muffler I have to wear.

Woman
can't you understand I come from a stronger breed
of Vikings? We ate you people for breakfast.

(sniffle)

56th Street Dancing School

One very young girl / 10
inches of leg above the knee
and two boys. She

gloms on to the both of them.

I'm in Hair she says
that one hot musical of the young
and kisses them each with a cheek.

Idiots
is the sign
        the idiot shakes at them
and they latch him into their hug

read—IDIOTS FOR THE CIA
across the girl's rump.

Outside
the snow is 2 feet high.
that's why / tho
        there's sun up in the sky
        they get together.
It's the weather.

Foolishness

Let me make a garland for my friends
so few in number,

and in the memory fewer still
casualties

of all Freud's terminology
dustbins.

And of my former self: ascetic
controller,

no rights to make a garland for them
(except

that it be a circle
around my own head.)

THE HAWK-FOOT POEMS

Hawk-foot's Guggenheim

Hawk-foot turns in the circle of joy.
Do not speak.

Hawk's neck an ankle of feathers.
"Speak to us Hawk-foot."

No lips above, no mouth. The letters
are hawk-foot-toes are pinfeathers.

Up and down, smiling toes
"I do not speak.   I dance."

Hawk-foot turns in the hallway
key in the mailbox
lock/don't speak.

Wife of Hawk-foot, the ridge-elk
"Wapiti, why do you speak?"

Hawk-foot turns in the circle of joy.
Do not speak.

The special de
livery letter is hawk-foot-toe is a pinfeather.

Ridge-elk turns in the circle of joy
Wapiti with two legs shorter.

Don't speak.
They don't speak.   They dance.

Hawk-foot Speaks

What can I say about Indians
that is not beautiful:

a wrist
ringed with feathers, old
Indian women sitting in the dust,
smoke-signals & rough blankets.

Hawk-foot says: you are a fool
white man/kiss my foot
and stop poking around.

I go on a bus to the reservation
sometimes, I go in a car.
Hawk-foot
goes on his own two legs;

what is the secret?

But
what can I say about Indians
that is not beautiful…

Shit-head-fool of a white man,
    it is the legs
    where the legs end
either way.

Hawk-foot Long Distance

There are mountains and plains between us
there are rivers.

There are government pamphlets
there are other reports.

There are horses flying
in the night sky
over boulevards & hogans

over Southern Asia:
Chevron Horses exploding in the sky at night.

Hawk-foot has eyes in his head
to see across oceans, sees
into Southern Asia:

charred hearts
smoldering in the fields.

How can I look with Hawk-foot?
How can I see?

Look into the poem also—
the poem also
has eyes.

Hawk-foot Brings Gifts

This
is the war-bundle.
This is the new hat

I told you about / keeps
the sun
from falling into your eyes

(they both do that).
This war-bundle
is full of words, scenarios

poems & directions
for talking about things
endlessly.

This last gift has
no connection with the other two:
it is useless,

a basket.
This last gift
is most difficult
to accept.

Hawk-foot Hunts Hawks

This is a bird
against which there is no denying
freedom.

He is culpable
    is a female

in his tricks
much in the way a wife becomes
tricky
when all else fails.

But a wife as a bird in Hawk-foot's house
is a blessing.
is a Joan or a Miriam,

a feathered, breathing emblem.
This is to say of Hawk-foot
who hunts hawks is culpable.

This is to say of the hunt:
VICTORY.

PIG/S BOOK

For a sow lies in the gutter or on the manure as if on the finest feather bed. She rests safely, snores tenderly, and sleeps sweetly, does not fear king nor master, death nor hell, devil or God's wrath, lives without worry, and does not even think where the clover may be. And if the Turkish Caesar arrived in all his might and anger, the sow would be much too proud to move a single whisker in his honor… And if at last the butcher comes upon her, she thinks maybe a piece of wood is pitching her, or a stone… The sow has not eaten from the apple, which in paradise has taught us wretched humans the difference between good and bad.

—Martin Luther

Pig

The pig does
what is important to the pig
& the chickens likewise. That's wallowing & squawking.

The horse has
an erection *so big* it isn't important
(turn away.

But what of the pig goes to market
to market to buy a fat horse who
does that.

& what else does a pig do?

Horse

The horse comes along
the fence, sidles
up to me. O what big ears, you
are a mule
(he goes away)

This time
he is shorter and shaggy and
there is a dog on his back.
I notice the ears— longer
His attempted whinny
—A donkey

The horse never convinces anybody
about anything. OINK / the dog

was the pig.

Cow

The job of the cow's to give milk
as the job is defined

by the man who takes
care of the cow as the job is defined.

Pig gives
gracefully of all he has,

neither is there snort
or crying.

Out in the fields the cow
remains, swishing the sun in.

Nor is there Pig,
but soft mooing.

Rabbit

The rabbit is all white meat
what you
eat on his thigh. In a pig's

eye of the rabbit
another (color of reds & black-orange)

and snout. Oh
cut that part off
poke out the eye. The rabbit

was meant to satisfy.

Sparrow

The sparrow
falls dead from the tree. Pig eats him / feh!
feathers, he

vomits and shakes all over.
Should the pig have known
better?

/

Consider.
Sparrow fell dead
from the tree.

Chicken

Cluck cluck, the chicken to
a safe place. The sky

the sky is falling.
Pig waits it all out, rain crap or snow
while / o sing

cluck cluck
the chicken makes a duck
under the barn.

Cat

Attention: this
is the pig speaking what I could tell

you beware of the cat/s
eyes in your house. Cat likes

coming down on your back
up where you can/t get him. Big

cat if your house is the jungle. Otherwise
little cat. Your house is

little.
oink

Bull

Furl of red—a cape of course
or an old shirt,
sweat maybe. You can picture

one running nameless across the field, where
Bull sits
red eye

& red penis
magnificent
by its size alone / back

where he can't see it. This is convenient:
he would chase it
getting nowhere. Could

Bull wear a red shirt?
Pig does.

Frog

Will die carelessly, always
from mawkish water, in poems
unreal

garden (wherein
                    a pig walks) &
on his back
with hand across chest (Chaplin-
esque) or like a dead

dancer—tap, or a comic says Layton. There
should have been hundreds
of frogs, or even pigs. There are.

It doesn't matter the joke is
silent / suck
of the pig entombs him . unreal

garden.

Hawk

Who lives at the tops of bald mountains / it is
the hawk
no nonsense.

And the farmer is out to get him
and the pig is
too.

Getting chickens and after that
getting scared
hawk eye.

And chipmunks and squirrels and gophers
a rabbit
and scared.

This hawk is as blind as a pig
as a bat takes up residence
in a cave.

Dove

The dove wings
tarnished
            under a gray cloud/or
clouds over the barnyard.
And the dove is rocking there
or dove-tailed. Pig

sings then of the dove, ripples
of skin on his back, and moves his bowels
such acts that make him hungry.

"I sing then of the dove, be it white
or otherwise tarnished,
(I am hungry.)

of small wings, 5
fingers in each wing
dove-tailed, for holding"

(and the dove has two feet
fingers in each foot
for holding)

Pig sings
of the dove, and follows him
his eyes in the air—

quick
flare of the nostrils.
He ripples the skin on his back

for holding,
and goes again
hungry, and moves his bowels.

Fox

Allow of the message in a strange language
that the fox is cunning
and sometimes wistful.

shhh
    moans the fox. cluck/shhh
    cluck fears the chicken
    (this is wistful)

and Pig shall wait there, beyond what
understanding beyond
wistfulness.

shhh/cluck is the wind
winter leaves
lift

up a thousand sparrows
or doves
in the wake of the fox.

And the pig
waits.

There
are teeth, are beaked heads / wild
eyes spinning / is the wind

shhh

        /

cluck, the fox.

And the Pig shall wait there
uncertain cock
of his head. And moans/so wist-
ful is the language
of the fox.

Skunk

By the road side and under tall grasses
where I walk upon it
both feet. Saith

the skunk is zebra
or a kind of cabbage,
horse

it is and with stripes a cat, tho
broad of tail. Woman
and where she walks

defines her. You are not woman,
but the skunk to me
asserts itself / names

itself. Skunk you are
at close range and beauty.

There is no mistaking this,
there is no
pig in it.

Lizard

Pig tells an old tale
and writes an old book

about a lizard
who doesn't move
& just sits there.

Pig squats in the shade
and writes
a book about a lizard

who sits in the sun
and watches the pig write
in the shade.

Flies

The flies are everywhere
like love is
everywhere hidden.

You wouldn't know it, they
rattle the corn husk bier.
They live in the pig/s ear.

Horse
stands head to ass for use of the other's
tail. Getting shed of the flies
he discovers the smell of love.

Once was a fly made love to an elephant
not a pig.

Mastery over hate
the way of the pig lives.

Buzzz/ are you hard of hearing?
Nobody loves the pig.

Pig takes the only way out.
He loves the flies.

Sheep

The lion lays down with the lamb
at the sea shore, where
Pig
on a holiday comes upon them.

The scene is ridiculous—Pig
standing and watching.

But this is a Holiday
and Pig does a jig
for them / there's

applause from the lion, blank
stare of the lamb (
a holiday.

Should winter come
Pig/s in a wool coat—
business as usual.

Worm

The worm is of two minds
and two bodies.
Should you

cut him in 4 parts
he will be that many—heads
and abilities.

oink this is philosophical
says Pig preening
and cleaning his nostrils

(worm/s
moving out
in one direction)

oink this is rhetorical—quick
curl of the tongue.
Where has the worm gone?

Follow that Pig.

Buzzard

Two pigs converge in a yellow wood,
jungle by another name. A buzzard
in the tree above them.

1st pig wears flowers.
Sleek and Oink is the other.
There is a buzzard.

There isn't any news.
I love you says pig one.
No news.

Buzzard does a bird
thing with his feathers,
shakes

down leaves dressing
pig 2.
I love you

says the other.
Sweet
meat says the buzzard.

Goose

What the goose says
is known to all around him:
Quack

says the goose
like the sharp slap of Pig/s ear
against pig head (all heads

might turn to it) Q u a c k, and the farmer
who is known as
Hick: having the awkwardness,

simplicity to understand
what the goose says
and turn to it.

But at night there is Pig only
awake, and steaming.
Hick

says the gander
cooing his feathers up,
coming on to the goose whispering

obscenities. *Moo*
says the gander. *Grrrr/* fear not the pig/s
telling

hick
is the farmer/*oh*
snort

Duck

The duck gets lost in the goose,
the likeliness of his bill,
a trick

of evolution
defined in weights and measures
a trick of the farmer's scale.

Quack you are making it rigid."
          (a shudder of wings
out of sleep)

Pig rages in the barnyard
in the likeness
of a boar,

ill-wind of the ducks around him:
vestigial wings of the eagle
talons of a condor.

A wind in the coiled tusks,
a fear of the placid duck.
Beware

of the silent animal
whose memories
extend.

Mouse

The mouse gets
into everything
and who can question his entrance,
grain

upon grain he takes
from the pig's trough / pieces
of straw from the horse's.
Pig

tho eats with his eyes open
has no control
of his jaw / chomp
of the mouse's livelihood

and sometimes chomp of the mouse.
If there's one thing
he doesn't like it's the taste of a rodent's
bowels / Pig

has no control.
Mouse takes his chances,
these
are occupational hazards.

Dog

A couple are very strange.
1 is the dog / has
a tail for the flies,

he is a friend to the horse.
The other
is Pig again,

could open bottles
by spinning.
There

are 3 burgundy, 5 rot-gut, 2
of strange mixture
and 1 scotch

(he drinks too much)
The first was an eater of table-scraps
and is domesticated.

Pig
circles his tail
nor escapes it.

Fish

When Pig takes up
stance against the night—curl of the tail
tusks
        of some imagined boar

and snort / what
can the fish do about it
deep in the brackish water?

O nothing. But
eating tadpoles, one has escaped
comes to the barnyard as some

imagined frog, mud puppy
or lungfish

        talks to the boar
the boar to the frog
and the two take up stance
against the night.

Bear

The pleasure of his company
is taken when he sleeps
and from a distance.

A cave
embittered in moss rock.
A pig

embittered in the ways
his life takes / as if
in a dream,

a hibernation.
Bear
is not called Smokey.

But the pig says "I am not dreaming,
a knife in the throat
a hammer." Come summer

Bear rises up
while the other
snorts.

This pig is no more
than a dream of a dark cave.

This bear
walks among people.

Elk

Stealth
among hard rock
                    (a brute isolation)

Pig keeps
snout to the ground
and out of trouble.

A Red Hat
a movement like leather,
like *steel.*

Elk
has not the ability
to smile

Mink

A fine coat in a fine store
highly desired—
purring.

Beautiful cages, and
choice grain.
A sharp knife

a clean smack on the head
gas / or
maybe even poison.

To be hung by the feet
to see it
coming that way—

I hate you
a football
a cheap purse.

Goat

Remember this Goat to the Pig,
for far away glances and everything
gathered together & eaten.

Everything Goat has eaten
Pig has considered, as
has the whole barnyard:

as chicken
longs to put beak
to the neck of the farmer.

Goat spent hours alone
digesting
while Pig was thinking

of hen's eyes beyond
the henhouse
beyond these fences.

Will
Goat be missed? Pig
will consider it.

Snake

Bright ringed and beautiful
coral, dry
and death rattle in a pig/sty
and in the belly of a pig,
dead. Yet

you are beautiful, ringed
turn of the wrist
whole arm in the belly of a pig.

And snake does walk out, turns
winter to spring
in a pig/s
eye fixed upon nothing.

The power that snake has
that pig should love him.

Birds

Birds fly south across the barnyard:
an omen. Pig thinks & wishes
he had a shotgun. Birds

flying in all directions
and everywhere. Ugh, says Pig—
so many ladders, black cats, strange smells, there

are omens and dreams, black wings and tusks.
O when
and will the birds come down.

They will
from everywhere, and do
build a nest in the dead pig/s nostrils.

Coyote

Coyote makes a diary of sadness
in the mountains, deserts
and plains where he lives

alone, and he sings from it.
At night,
even where Pig can hear,
it moves

in and across Pig/s eyes
and in pig/ears, near
where his brain

ticks: what they will do is make
meat of me
bacon and chops
a-roast-pig, and whatever else is

tasteful. Coyote

sings from it.
and Pig hears it

alone, in the barnyard
where he lives.

POEMS 1970

The Gear

We packed it up with care:
    old tennis shoes for going thru the stream,
some Hershey bars, an ounce of salt in plastic,
matches, and some powdered food,
                          then set off in the dark.

The first few miles are flat, thru woods
a porcupine, some bulls, and then
the sign:
        no 4 legged animals beyond this point,
and start on up.
              The time
in 66, when Fred came with us (Geologist
from Berkeley)
                 brought such crazy gear
we laughed: small umbrellas
for the ankles, keeps the dew off
good, plastic tube-tents for the rain,
a folding Boy-Scout knife,
Jello Gelatine
to drink/still warm —some energy,
                and found a use for all of it.

But this time, earlier, in 65
it starts to rain
when we have reached the first ascent: a tangled
low growth forest, over rock.

It's wet, I get
a foot up
        on a root, that's sliding in the arch
and hang by thread of vines

a hundred feet or more
of sloping rocks

below
        the waterfall, where me and Larry climbed
4 years ago, and never found our way,
had lost the trail, gathered trees
and burned them
                in the woods all night.

From where I look now
holding by the root
                the water running under it
                                the boot
could be a slipper—thread of life.

In 69,
at New Paltz where the gear
was ropes and pitons (Tony
                having brought a book
                about their use) & I was

fat and out of shape, that year, we watched
the young man
climbing on the rock, by toes and nails,

sheer face
        from where we stood, above
100 feet, two legs, his girl's, hanging
off the cliff.
            The rope between her legs
he wasn't holding,
kept on going
up, then
        UP-SIDE DOWN, the L shaped overhand,

and when he reached her gave a *whoop*,
stood up
        straight along the face
        2 feet below the top, and spread his arms.

Her legs then gathered round his waist
and pulled him in,

the rope between their legs
unused: a thread of life.

It's 65 and Robert's
slipping in his pack.

We all fall down a couple times
in mud. Paul keeps
the gear intact.

It's getting clear.
We're up 12000 feet,
the timbers very thin
the air
        is thinner still. We talk about our lungs, and how
we do this every year,

then head up to Pierre:
5 lakes above the timber-line.

And when we get there, take our packs off,
feel so light
        but awkward, almost
falling forward
            from the missing weight
            then get our legs,
                eat, & look around.

That night
we sleep beneath a moon
incredible, at this height
no timber, only
                    rocky basin.

What we brought
is tucked around me: 65
to 69, UPSIDE DOWN,
a Porcupine, a Boy-Scout-Knife,
water rushing, Tennis Shoes, *beyond this point*
a Root.

Boot-like Slippers Ropes & Pitons,
Plastic Tubes, Hersheys
Bulls. Umbrellas
Energy

…and we were
coming up. Such burdens on our backs,
the air's too thin
to tie things up together, but connected.

When we stopped to breathe,

above us on the ridge
a Stand of Elk
who live up there
just
      looked at us a while
then walked away:

their gear
was growing from their heads.

Camera (1946)

old men sit
in the spaces of lost energy
           under
eucalyptus, reluctant
to move, but
do
   /

        their heads turn. My
grandmother stands, rests
on her cane.
           Pigeons
light on her shoulders, her hands
at the mission
San Gabriel.

Provincetown: Short-Suite

1
passion passion passion
the young
       walk the streets of P-Town
AC?DC. You
see & can't put words upon them

be they
happy or sad or merely
       saddened by what they see
of those who watch them
       and of each other.

One
is trying to dance
in the street, stiff-armed & awkward.

Only
the Gays have rhythm
enough, or the Hare Krishna dancers,
being professional.

       The boy
friend of the one who's dancing
tries dancing too.

Young men
watch them & laugh.

Old ladies
fear them, thinking them free:

it is not so.
Would that it were.

2–Cycle

Gulls scratch on the roofs peak
Flickers
hammer it home—4 poles
marking the land,
nobody
makes the grass grow,

certainly:
blackberries down Pamet Road.
Oysters,
on the flats at Wellfleet:

>   …saw
>   many gulls at low tide,
>   (few people)
>   jelly fish getting at clams.

Up to our knees, crabs
pinching our toes
taking what they can get—we

rake & steal, bringing it home

never enough:

peat-moss and cheap seed.
Mulch it, water it good.

No chance. Even
over the Orleans nursery:

grackles grackles grackles

3–Airforce Station

Crab-apple tree in the backyard
one side eaten away
by wind.
      Waiting in rain for the last train
in an empty station. The headless
body of a bird
         in damp grass. A dead
rabbit in the basement: bits of fur
        holes
the size of half-dollars
in his side.
Teeth Marks.

You can see three domes from certain points
along Route 6, and elsewhere,
squat and close to the ground:
what are they for?

And sometimes
thru binoculars, have picked the trails of jets
out of mare's-tails
and the planes themselves
like Hawks
      in a moving hover.

Catbirds sing in the afternoon.
You never see them.

You see the cat
sits quiet in different places.

They don't wear uniforms
but on their windows
    cartoon birds in the centers of bull's-eyes
fat and smiling, carrying
no lightning bolts no weapons.

The cat has a soft body
and purrs continually,

stretches and yawns
in different places

    : every morning every morning
bodies of dead animals
around the house.

4

It rains, and then the sun comes out
and then it rains again
and then it stops.

It's evening—Sparrows
pecking in the stones—Night Hawks
hover in the air
and dive.

The cat
who thrives these days
on rabbits, squirrels and mice
sits in the grass, and is

oblivious
of the hawks I see
thru new binoculars, each color
and their beaky heads
and eyes.

In Provincetown
there's rain upon the streets
where people walk—They
rub together on die dock—The young men
find each other
and go off together.

Those just newly in
and those alone
gather on the benches in the square,

the one-legged cyclist passes on his TR6.
The air
whistles thru his plastic knee.

Sparrows
peck among the stones.

5–*Waltz*

The women lie upon the beach.
Because the men have not
         forgiven them their sex
they lie together

at the nexus, where
         the foreshore cuts the beach

and poke their fingers in the sand
or read a book.

The beach is full of men
who lie together and believe
     the women are immoral

     and they reach
inside each other's heads
for love.

     And there are flies.
     and there are fishermen in boats.
     and when the sun is highest—
     lotions
          stroked into the body.

And when the sun goes down
they climb the dunes
that run along the beach—

the men, the lonely women:
each to each.

6–Dolphins

Somehow, living
          not in their own water, the Dolphins
            blow in the darkened tank.
Evening.

Sea washing against concrete, over
a pile, a cluster of piles, buoys
          where vessels are moored
in the open water:

they call such structures
Dolphins, the way
          they hold against the sea.

Someone
is walking along the shore, eating
amphetamines.
               And farther back,
around the fudge shops on the pier
the young
are holding close to one another
smoking
          marijuana, when they can.
The language: ups & downs
yellow
      jackets on the fishermen
with flags up
docking, with their Bass & Flounder,
lay them out like banners on the pier.

The Dolphins
somehow live & blow
and roll their bodies in the tank
and speak.

In Corpus, past the West-Gate Tower
& bar in which a Texan
knifed a sailor in the cheek (the workings
          of his jaw laid open
to the bone) I took Marie

a Wave, to Padre Island, couldn't
make it with her.
               We had driven
in the night across the beach

had almost
   run a sailor down
was sleeping on the sand.

I couldn't speak to her
about my fear / drank beer
   and rode back in the morning,
bragged about
as how I'd layed her, to my friends.

   They speak: it is a certainty,
   not English

(or the way
his hand came up
against the headlights, and the brakes—
no squeal, but biting sickly
in the sand, the girl
laughing
   at my side, the beach
so wide and flat I couldn't tell
just where the Gulf began)

   but words.

The fishermen
lock up their boats: the Dolphin
Sand Shark & The Viking
   and go home.
The boys
have put their hands
upon the girls, who are high
enough, and smiling.

Everything seems clearer to him
(speeds) every star
electric and the breeze,
each subtle changing motion, knows
before he comes upon him
tho it's darker
by the tank.

Not hand in hand, but furtive
till they reach his place
        then do it with the lights on.

We know
they are intelligent, believe
that they have tried to speak to us
as much
        as we have tried
to speak to one another, think

that we have proved it
in a tank:
        have made them
splash around
and bring us plastic rings.

The girls
slip off their jeans, the whiteness
of their asses. Fishermen
are drinking beer
                and thinking
how they'd like to screw
one of these hippy kids. The boys

get naked too, and joke
as how the water's full of sharks

and how they'd better
stay here on the sand.

      They fumble
      till he holds him round the hips,

and when he comes
he thinks he makes a sound like Dolphins
who are laughing.

Crazy

Sometimes, in spite of death
or biography,
          I am crazy
for the sweet earth on which we live.

Where go from that, except
to Russ's Ram
who falls upon his knees and lets
the dog tear pieces off his rump
for food.

    Would
    that each of us
    could understand the need
    of others,
          give
    our bodies as a feast
    of life—

and in this way
I pick up feathers
that the cat has left, and use them
on your body,
          think
of everyone I meet
that we could put our mouths
upon each other—

sometimes
I am crazy for that Ram

    that he adores the earth
    the way his haunches open to the sky

the way the dog takes
pleasure from his silence

(think

if we are good,
like him,
the ground will let us in).

Cold House

There are those who make love in poems
others
        send letters of great vehemence
to those who are making love
or writing poems about it.

I am one of those.
And yet
as I enter the cold room
        find you
sexless, sitting before the cold fire
dressed in old clothes
        trying
to take the chill off, I

find I am coming
as if for the first time
into your presence.

That's why
I go into the other room, write
letters to those who are making love,
search for
        "what is wished for
realized in the 'dream' of the poem."

Which is simply, sometimes
        just seeing you
I enter newly
into my life.

VECTORS

Justice Justice
to the sound of music:
the trees are alive
the people
turn back to the Law,

Sing: don't walk on the grass,
on the people's heads,
Property Property

to the sound of music
the hills are alive
the people
turn back to the Law,

Justice Justice

In Kafka Country

When his outlook is optimistic
the results are always negative,

and vice versa. K
enters a town he expects is friendly
then can't find his way about.

O
enters into strange pacts
with people he has never seen
and does not care about.

In the summer he goes away west
looking for people to deal with.
In the fall he comes back again
having discovered America.

O   spends his time at Mt. Rushmore,
The Bad Lands, Jewel Cave
Forest Lawn & Disneyland.

K   opens a door in the city
and is arrested.

Out in America people eat white bread
or don't eat at all.   O

returns east with the sentence.
K   wonders
what was the crime?

Vectors *(for Sara)*

We go one place coming from another
It is that simple.

Looking
for L we are going

on rapid transit.
We are going—
        —it is like
        the quarter horses I told you about
        go only in one direction,
        the man who turns them.

We are plodding, our feet are bleeding
up this hill

we pass
the skulls of animals & humans
        …is like
        the cows I told you,
        bred with short legs to fatten them,
        moved in the fields with trucks.

I write this down I write this down.
It is another lie.
We go one place coming from another.

By the Sea By the Sea / 1

In the morning
or afternoon

the wisdom of pelican over the wake
ignored by the bathers, and
the fish also,

whose beak
can hold more than his bellycan-
gull eye & slow wing.

What hold we ourselves in the summer
biting off more than we can
our noses to spite, etcetera?

Our eyes
are bigger than we can hold. The stores
provide
thousands of rubber things

we hold to the crowded sand,
while the pelican
makes his awkward dive / holds
what he can hold

and bends seaward—
is as wisdom.

By the Sea By the Sea / 2

It is simply the green water
shifts
      the brown kelp
sea-lettuce, the lost raft

is rubber—
rolls on itself.

surf clams.
a sand bar.
one
Mediterranean woman, her child.
others.

Sand
shifts the blue water
green kelp

wind/ she
holds the child's face.

the lost raft
gone.

By the Sea By the Sea / 3

Board floats on the deep water
past the bar—
he sits.

sun spots.
no wind.

no breeze lifts the blanket
moves
      your brown skin.

salt.
sand.
     I thirst
is when I wake you,

Miriam.

By the Sea By the Sea / 4

The bread is stone,
and the stones
     are as various as shells.

The shells
are sea-birds rising
             a mile off.

The sea changes.
The sand
changes.

Under
the sand is hard rock.
The rock is animal.

By the Sea By the Sea / 5

In her arms:
flowers as bright as any sun.

Across this water: war
in the eye that sees that far,
or is blind.

Only
that the eye stops
sometimes short of it.

Which explains nothing—
nor is justice
love
or any magnitude.

Only
is the way she carries
a thing that lives.

By the Sea By the Sea / 6

Fish in the water.
a world of fish,
where the line enters.

We
see only the fishermen,
sea-birds, the periwinkles,
stone & sand.

Grey
day turns pink.

Where the line enters,
the water now
red streaked.

A pelican.

Where the line enters
the world of fish.

No fish.
2 suns.

Poem for My 30th Birthday

When I was one and twenty
I loved very many
It was a very good year.

at 30, tho dirty,
it/s hind
sight. Could

not would
life
 /
wife

The Other

I speak to my friends of things
impossible to name (no
serviceable items)
                    a quality of air to frame
the way it is outside.

And it's all right.
In friends we have a common ear.

But when the girl comes to be serviced
(and how can you name her as that kind of friend?)
there is another in the room.
You say "I want to forget him,"
surprised that he still exists,
                    to find that

it is you there
come with the words
always these words of no
sufficient use.

Tactical/Animal Science

they use dogs
they use horses

those
who track in the fields
with plows behind them
are useless

to them. it is
a dog with his tail down
to be kicked, coward
who wants to sit quiet
 among the flies—
unamerican.

the horses
are very strong and hard like iron
horses roar in the winter
among groups of people, their nostrils blowing.

the dogs
are very lean
though in kennels with warm food
and sleek coats.

the horses also have names.
they come when you call them.

—who have been trained
to act like human beings.

Spring Walk

Each day returns to the same
emptiness, be it
Spring again
or the coming of any season.

Earth-
day or week, still
Joan
     couldn't go it alone:
that liquor store / that neighborhood

...walked with her
black men eyeing us
birds in the trees

in Brooklyn?   well
pigeons, children
still young enough.

Spring again
could be winter. Joan
what hunger? We
walk, talking thru it
automatic

mechanical
words, drained back
to emptiness.

...said
Spring again. pigeons
Earth-day
passing
of any season.

The Gulf Stream

A sense
of being in bed so late this morning. 7:10
feels like
    the king sleeps in
been getting out so early lately
6:45, on 57th Street
smiles on the early workers
counting the change in Horn & Hardart,
assistant managers
window washers.

20 degrees, but
nobody fucking my beard—
'morning brother'.

Quarter of 8, the painter
coming to touch the ceiling up,
me in my bathrobe watching.

(He's short) just
a little job, I say—
the hostile look, turns to a joke
    I like this guy
he's German
about 50.

So—
he works. We talk
of the weather, insurance rates, inflation,
avoid
the president's policy,
keep to such neutral ground.

We understand each other, tho
he slips
calls me Mrs. once,
apologizes: *been working for women*
so much lately

               ...my wife
wants to go to Florida
she don't understand
I got my work in The City
or the Gulf Stream
that it's turning

ya know
in ten years New York
'll be a summer resort

upstate
fish coming certain time of the year? you
ain't got it no more

can't tell if you got summer or winter
or what anymore

       (a summer resort?)

I heard it on tv
things gonna be good here in ten years.

my wife
she don't understand sometimes.

me too.

Messing Around

The word in my life
is what I want to sing about.
Today

is Saturday again, when
I usually watch the ball-game
    or do some work
        or simply mess around:
like going out on the terrace I recently have.
My cat comes with me, probably
thinking we'll
do some messing around the shrubbery:

    my meager weeds,
    I call them plants, still thriving tho
    it's mid-November.

My neighbor
has a different girl on his terrace every night,
and a fire now that it's cold
made out of logs they deliver
wrapped in fine paper,
at 80 dollars a cord:

    money
    is not what I need so much, but
    some simple joy in the world these days,
    being so far up
              over the street.

Paul's downtown.
Byrd's in the decent country. Carl's

probably in some similar bag,
freezing his ass in Wisconsin.
So—
I have these weeds, their
simple need to grow,
and have my cat today
sitting
as if in a garden.
Well,
I'll go inside
                    (my neighbor's current girl
singing some gentle song
comes thru the walls to me)
and go downstairs for cigarettes
which I don't need, but
to find some word,
        and step in the narrow store.

Viceroys, I say.
He's new:
you can tell by the way
he wears his flowered shirt:
        on a wintery day
        of *summer* flowers: a Puerto Rican man
oblivious of the stares,
and warm
            in that summer shirt.

Bis-er-oys, he says
and finds them quick.
I've
only got a five,
but it's amazing how he makes out change,
and with that PR flair,
counting in Spanish.

He turns to the other customers,
and I'm
back on the street again:
    winking at everyone I pass
    and giggling like a fool.

Now
what can I make of this I think?
I'll look it up
Viceroy: a person
appointed to rule a country
…American butterfly
who mimics the monarch in coloration
    (could be some heavy thoughts about
    the state of the nation)
but
Bis-er-oy— on what could be
a cold, sad Saturday afternoon
in mid-November, I'm
sitting by the window now
in my flowered shirt & Indian hat
awaiting my wife
who's gone to some other store
for groceries.
           She'll
laugh to see me dressed like him:
a butterfly.

Some
simple joy in the world I said
and in the people
that give us warmth
& random pleasure,
and pass it on to my wife
and to my cat

        and neighbor
to give them joy in any weather
and simple pleasure
mucho.

THE WRESTLERS
& OTHER POEMS

THE WRESTLERS

Gorgeous George

He wore
gold bobby-pins in his hair,
and raised turkeys

in California
years before the Olympic Stadium was air conditioned,
and old ladies swilled beer and yelled and sweated.

In the ring he would prance and strut
like a turkey, and say
"mess up my hair and I'll kill you."
But they always did it, escaping
barely with their lives.

His specialty
was the Flying Mare.

He was a gentleman
in his golden briefs and curled locks,
and yet he was dainty.

Each Christmas
he gave away 500 turkeys
to orphan homes.

This was before
gays were openly common
in California.

Antonino Rocca

Argentina. The Pampas. Green Mansions.
The Bola.

And came to this country
with the strength of two ballet troupes.

He was a clean man, "hit
weed de flat de han"
(but his *feet*). Once

I saw him catch a man by the ears
using only his toes.
It was miraculous.

And would do cartwheels and great spinnings
around the ring. His end

came thus unbidden,
landing
with the turn-buckle between his legs.

It didn't injure his feet,
but it took his spirit away.

Mr. Moto

A rose petal in a finger bowl, a wisp
of mushroom in clear soup.
going shoeless,
the nails are manicured.

This one has suffered
every indignity
from the eye gouge, to having
his middle finger bent back almost to the wrist,

and is
a master against such torment.

There is a woman
who remembers the concentration camps of California,
opens the ropes for him,
burns incense / goes through
preparations mildly reminiscent of Samurai.

At the bell
there is a feigning like Judo, like
"Death to American Swine."

In the role of *the yellow peril* he loses
often enough.

He has been educated in this country.

He remembers
concentration camps in California.

The Masked Marvel

Could I have told you his name
it would have been the end of him.

Imagine
that he might have worked in a car wash
and practiced
by thwacking a chamois over the hoods

or was a banker.
Sometimes
you'd think him a priest, so carefully
with open palms / breaking
out of initial clinches.

Nobody
took him seriously / too much
theatricality, in holding a delicate ear.

A has-been
Shakespearean actor, an injured
labor-leader in his protestations,
or a priest again.

His mask
had stars on the side, and was the kind we wore
at Halloween,
a little bit small, inadequate

around the eyes, so that he couldn't see too well
and took to groping
around the ring.

Who was this masked man, who
might have become a fine doctor or a lawyer?

His trunks
were a little tight / the stars
were set in a field of blue. Maybe

he was someone you knew.

The Dwarfs

whose names I can't remember,
who cannot be explained by science,
who in their mad tumblings
brought people to their feet,
who could not possibly have lived
anywhere
but in California,
whose heads are misshapen,
whose eyes are the blankness of stone,
who spin,
who never expected to be taken seriously
by anyone.

    A Dwarf's face looking out of a well.
    A Dwarf in a dark closet.
    Dwarfs
    waiting, under a bridge.
    The Snow White Dwarfs.
    The Fierce Dwarfs of Tolkien.
    The Mad Dwarf of Lagerkvist.
    Dwarfs helping a scientist.
    A Dwarf trapped in the cold stone of a brooch.
    Dwarf Star.

The Mad Dwarfs were spinning in the ring,
oblivious
of the people.

    There were no people.
    There were no Dwarfs.
    There was only the referee:

Primo Carnera
bewildered among Dwarfs.

What could a man like Carnera have expected,
turning to wrestling? He could never
have expected this.

What can I expect from my memory?
What do you expect from me?

There was—
Primo Camera.
There were—
Dwarfs spinning around him.

What can I tell you?

This is not about talent.
That belongs on a job application.

The Garibaldis

A father and son team.
So many
possibilities of a tragic end.

Leo
is having his arm torn off
by Wild Red Berry,

while Gino
is passionately concerned
with getting away from Mr. Moto.

Wild Red had said
he would drive Leo
through the mat of the El Monte Legion Stadium,

and the crowd,
though initially scornful,
is having its doubts.

But now,
as if in a miracle
Gino remembers the judo-chop

and turns it against his foe.
He effects the rage of Leo,
and the rest is denouement.

Gino
when asked at the interview
the cause of the final success:

"The father protecta the son."
It's an old Italian custom.

Lord Blears

He sits in a garden.
he wears a monocle.

In a garden in England where Rupert Brooke might have
declaimed poetry
standing, in a garden a great distance
from world war one.

Sometimes
like in world war one he is being choked to death
by foreign powers, his monocle
spinning at the end of its golden chain.

By Baron Leone
with incredible crassness, like a rosary
he plucks at the Lord's nose.

A Duke
a Count a Lord an Anglican
canticle so austere
it gives rough comfort to the ear.

Our Blears,
tho he shall turn the Baron on his hip,
with glazed eyes

sees pages
he turns with the ends of his delicate fingers
of lost poets
encased in the wood of England.

He belongs in the heat of a garden,
gently sweating.

Wild Red Berry

What he never made was
good sense
or a lot of money.

Picture
a tight fist pounding a table
2 small fists pounding a table,

a fury
so transparent it was believable.
We always

believe in such things—
a man pushed to such extremity
just has to be successful.

Wild Red
sat at a table
pounding out victories

he never won.
Men sit around tables;
we always believe them.

Chief Don Eagle

Incredible Indians moving across the plains at dusk.
Arizona Highways. Bullets

Pale-faced Indians on a Painted Desert.

Dead Indians in a creek bed,
pathetic
useless arrows & bows.

A young man comes to the city
with a hair cut
like you have never seen
(9 Indians starve on the reservation)

Meanwhile:

one Indian up in the city
in the wake of the semi-final,
a war dance, and
war whoops of the sound of 10 voices ringing
through the stadium.

This is the Indian of our fears
and of our guilts:
a young man / a fool
before his time,
                with a Mohawk
        haircut
        like any yokel, yet
he is tricky: his holds are ancient
rituals, and successful.

Chief Sitting Bull
Chief Crazy Horse
Chief Big Heart

Chief Don Eagle:
in the ring a razor of hair,
in a place where his face should be
    A Medal of Honor
      The Legion of Decency.

This
is the measure of his success:
we lay our money down
like Greeks

against our fears, and guilts.

Strangler Lewis

Call him The Grand Old Man
who, before this modern nonsense
took the measure of Stecher
and Jules Strongbow.

My uncle,
Joe Connelly himself a middleweight champ,
remembers The Strangler in the freight yards
squeezing a boxcar
spring under his arm.

The fear
men had of him was specific (the way
he came by his name
was literal) an old kind of fear

beautiful
in being justified. My uncle
would show me the middleweight belts he'd won
and brag

about his son
Forrest, who used to bite people in the leg,
and once woke him up with a hammer.

The box
my uncle kept his belts in was old and made of steel.
He was very tough

at 60, but
remembering The Man—
would turn his head away
and shudder. This

was Lewis
T h e S t r a n g l e r

Jonathan Edwards Compared to a Wrestler

He could be said to have struggled with sin
by wrapping his body around it,
taking its weight upon his own shoulders:
a Helicopter-Twirl
of what he believed
was sin in other people.

And in the arena at Enfield
he put it that way to the unconverted:
a full-nelson, possibly
a hip-roll,
        banging them very close
to the dreadful Pit of the glowing Flames
of the Wrath of God.

But the real opponents
were the demons he wrestled with in his own head,
one of them peaceful & kind, the other
bending his back like a bow,
causing his eyes to bulge.

This was a nightmare
dream of some unending tag-team match
in which he remained always
the weaker partner, with arm heavy as lead
reaching out of a hammer-lock
for those extended fingers.

And so like the tortured Sandor Szabo,
locked in a back-breaker, he protested the audience,
throwing his own burden upon them:

despicable Worms of the Dust...
Kings of the Earth before GOD are as Grasshoppers...
the Creature is made Subject
to the Bondage of your Corruption, not willingly;
the Sun don't willingly shine upon you...
the earth don't willingly yield her Increase
to satisfy your lusts.
O Sinner! Consider the fearful Danger you are in.

And at night he considered the fearful danger he was in,
locked in the grip of the dreadful hand,
carefully fighting the perpetual main event—
one fall & no time limit—*wrestling*
and conflicting with this almighty merciless Vengeance.

He could not be said to have won the match.
He could not be said to have lost it.

...who knows the Power of God's Anger?

The Ladies

Who is so delicate to move this way?
Thin dancers in a lighted pool,
Ginger Rogers spinning on some steps.

These are the ladies
I told you about. This man
who watches them,

     and this is the flying-head-scissors,
     this is the hair-throw.

These are the Gypsy ladies from a makeshift town
who fight because they are too old
and strong for loving.

Or else they dream of maidens in a swimming pool,
or else they are scorned by maidens,

     and this is the step-over-toe-hold,
     this is the hip-lock.

These are the pornographic ladies

I told you about
who wrestled in those pictures in my youth
wherein I learned of daylight
bursting from a tortured crotch.

The Current Champ

Bruno Sammartino does not exist,
is the current champ, alive
in the sad dreams of old ladies

in a place somehow revealed to the mind
as Madison Square Garden,
The Olympic Stadium

of Jules Strongbow and Gotch
Jim Londos
and The Strangler.

Lew Thez does not exist,
has a wife runs a health studio, is revealed
as the victim of pickpockets on a TV show.

In some place in the summer
The Strangler
rages in the freight yards.

Jules Strongbow
no longer exists.

Lew Thez
is Bruno Sammartino.

Care of the Wrestlers

Provide them with oils and velvet ropes.
Salve their incredible wounds.
Put them

on a beach somewhere on the coast of Africa
beside a jungle of harmless snakes.
Give them fruit.

Give them
the right to wear medals & sequins
bright steel belts and magnificent robes.

Let it be summer all year, let them
practice the reverse-suplex, the inside-
step-over-toe-hold, the full-nelson.

For the wrestlers
are gladiators without weapons, are ranters and ravers
for an hour only.

For they are gentlemen
in their profession, are twisted together
forming chains of daisies.

Twist them together
forming chains
of daisies.

for in their profession
they do no harm
to any man.

THE OTHER POEMS

The Rope

In the outside world
everybody dead in their tracks
rain for 3 weeks
logs won't burn

women
get vertigo on the street
there is nowhere you can walk straight for a mile

rain
could be falling on the moon
or across it, you
won't believe it when you get out

if you get out
from a chair
in a green room
tho unlike a throne.

Pellets
of cyanide lowered into a basin of acid.

     …it was a noose flung over a tree
     limb, to bring him down
     to proper stature: horse thief
     cattle were stomping in his shed
     the wrong brand
     on them, iron still
     hot in the fire…

Rain in the country
it falls on the beaches

rains over
the major cities,
this place to begin with, the Congress
a factor of budget
of breath / could be
your real blood on our hands.

   ...caught him
   without his boots, couldn't run
   from us, he
   gave that strange squeak
   from his throat we turned away from
   because we knew
   he knew, what was coming...

In the outside world, still
there is a kind of air to be breathed.

Jim, alias Bill
the news is
clam guts fester in the can
and rain, and

cat brings a mouse in to play, she
bats it in the head
it hops away, then
pounces at it

today
bird found
below the sodden bush

muskrat
dead along the pond.

...someone
accused him, who was not our leader
but the man injured
by him pulls the hat down
over, to save us
from his face...

I can see death so many times each day
where it's pure, in the wilderness
take part in it

even
the tongues of clams move,
touch my fingers
as I cut them up.

Each
blade of grass
cut down, each flower
is not ridiculous
if you eat it
if you make some use
out of it
      if there is some necessity
      in it
      for a good life.

I write poems
I grind out some version of existence
I think I'm in trouble
walking
against traffic
spinning
I imagine I'm strolling
under this dark sky

munching
your bones like bread sticks
in rain.

　　　…his own rope
　　　dry in the shed, waxed
　　　coiled up proper, no twists in it
　　　of 12 strands, used
　　　mostly for heavy work…

Clam gut,
what a smell it gives off,
tie it up
take it to the dump
gulls
ripping through the trash.
if anything lives.
　　　　　　　The man sits
　　　　　　　with a rifle
　　　　　　　shooting rats.

Jim
alias Bill
I send a letter
I read
letters to the editor,
dear sir
it's barbaric,

fear
everyone I see, imagine
I can change things go
to the voting box.

...hands tied
behind his back, a thin cord
somebody
brought with them, a sharp knife
to cut him down with...

Repair it somehow
take back what is done
the needle out
skin closing over
those stricken arms, your victims
dead from the jolt of insulin,
all those wives
and relatives
guilty
of money
you wanted
and took.

(or
if you didn't kill them)

We profess not
innocence,
but life, a

thick, strong cord
made of intertwisted strands
of fiber.
A ropelike string, as of beads.
To fasten or tie with a rope.
To mark off or enclose with...
to catch with a lasso.
Know the ropes.

To be acquainted with procedure.
Rope in. To entice. Persuade.

...he came along with the horses, whoever
pulled him. no moon
the rain stopped, somebody
made a fire
under it, bark
peeled from the groove
the rope made, crackled
in the flames...

...his own horse
poor wind, wheezed under
the weight, hunched down
knees gripping the leather. Rope
brought down over
his hat
crack
of a willow switch.
somebody.
the horse farts,
moves out...

In the outside world
were there still time
and air to breathe.

...it was a good rope.

Work

The work depends on
things utterly simple:

the way cheap nails
bend
     driving them in.

A man is only
     as good as his tools or
a man is better
or worse) than the tools he has purchased.

But the work gets done, the tools
need to be cared for.

Maybe the tools rust)
The man goes into the finished structure.

The tools do
or don't.

Ethology
for Paul

The song
has finally broken forth.
not spring. It's still November.

We wander, in
and out of the shops on the avenue.
Women
muffed in their ratty furs,
the style

of pigeons is to shit
when they take off
or are landing. At least

homing pigeon. In California.
a friend
told me how silly it looks
when they let them go in a distance race:

sometimes
a thousand pigeons
somewhere out in the desert.
Maybe ten people pulling the traps,
then running like hell
in a cloud of shit.

And the birds themselves, the
joyful, 'fuck-you' nature of their rising.
circle
and conical
cloud over the sand.

And over here—
where it's cold and everyone gruff and nasty
and whacking each other with bundles
and these ladies, in their
'I don't care, I'm cool' old fur coats, there's

this one fat pigeon
parked on an awning bar,

jumps off, with
a squat in the air before
his wings open.

one bit
of shit
trails down plop
on the fattest coat:

O/SHIT she says
and brushes it onto her glove, then
realizes what she's done,
then laughs out loud:

the song.

Incest

A young boy decides
he wants to go to bed with his mother,
who has given him
ample indication
that it's all right to do that.

And because the boy's mother
and father sleep in separate rooms, there's
no problem about the boy's going in
which he does one night
but in the morning they can't get separated.

It seems
the mother's vagina
has for some reason begun to expand
and started to pull the boy back inside her,
which creates a problem
because he is 10 years old.

But thank god he isn't a big boy
and the mother is able
to strap him to her body
with two of her husband's belts, tho
most of him is still outside of her
but if he hunches up in a ball
she can cover him with an old maternity dress.

Now the father is quite shocked
when he notices but the mother is very coy
and delicate and says she's been to the doctor that day
and that she's been pregnant for months.
She tells him their son
left just that morning for camp.

Now the marvelous thing
is that the father becomes very attentive again
to the mother after 10 years of ignoring her,
and begins to bring flowers and candy.
And the mother feels delicate and feminine
again, and the boy keeps moving inside her.

And then after 4 months
(of being fed in the bathroom
of close quiet talks with his mother
of hearing the tenderness between his parents)
even his head goes inside
and the father finally
goes away on a business trip and the mother
goes to an out-of-the-way hospital.

When the father comes back the mother
tells him about the miscarriage
but neither of them are too sad
and take great pleasure
in having their son home from camp.

From that day on
the father sleeps in the mother's bedroom,
the son takes
the bedroom his father has vacated
and begins to get interested in girls.

The Father

This is a very
traditional
          story about a father
who is cut from tin and a son
who has surely only
created this image of his father.

The mother
plays a very small part in this:
she helps
          the son carry
his father to bed at night;
she reminds the father to
go thru
          motions of eating at dinner time.

The father is truly
cut out of tin, and though he has hinges
at his knees and hips
from the waist up
he is very rigid
and his arms are only hinged at the shoulders.

The night before
the father takes the son out on weekends
the son creeps into the bedroom
where his father sleeps
and paints
          an appropriate smile
or grin on the flat surface of the father's face.

Now the son imagines
there is a real father
about, that he sleeps under the bed of the tin
father, and that he is rounded
like the son is,

but the son can't
                    look under there
afraid that what he imagines
might be true   The mother
plays a very small part in this
tho she tells him always
to sleep in the center of the bed.

One day
the father takes the son out in the country
and as long as he stands
with his flat body
cutting the wind
everything goes along fine.

But while they are walking
out of a wood and over a rise in a meadow
the son trips
and the father turns to help
him and is caught by the wind.

Now imagine how
the father reaches out to the son
as he is lifted
                    slightly off the ground.
He
picks up speed and is waving his legs
and stiff arms
to keep his balance. Think of the son

dumbstruck and helpless
running after
his father who misses the first trees
but is struck
by a hanging limb
and is ripped in half
                              at the abdomen:
the one sound the son hears—
the tearing of a piece of tin.

Now the mother
plays a very small part in this
and when the son gets home, she says:
where is your father?

        "I suppose he's hiding under the bed
again." And the mother says
well, be sure to sleep right in the center
of the bed tonight

and before the son goes to sleep
he begins to feel
his skeleton eating his flesh away
from the inside.

Accent

…weaving
& pressing against the bulkhead
                    like a pillar,
was Samson, stars
              bouncing off my head,
holding the wheel,
the big ship breaking
to windward. 3 days out
drunk,
        standing the mid-watch.

Himself
caught me at it,
the line of his mouth, under
a calm sky.
            Put down in his log:
the 1st mate was drunk tonight.

6 days out,
relieved from duty,
the big ship still
moved on a flat sea.

The 7th day,
passed Himself on the 2nd deck.
He turned away.

Wrote
down in my log:
tonight
the Captain was sober.

Lore

First the animals go
out in the night
on the grass or among the tall bushes. L
draws them.

We
choose the darkness also—
it is explained that
inhibitions, our past history,
mother
of night, we are afraid to look
at our naked bodies.

L is as strong in Senators,
Congressmen,
CIA, we accuse the President
of a dark mind.

What we can learn
is fur
is the hair on our heads, feathers
of dark wings. And L

passes thru fingers
even thru pens touched
to a document.

Whoever is afraid
of government
dogs
flying in the face
of convention on lawns in the suburbs,
it's all right,

is explained
that dogs, horses, those in the air
in the natural kingdom
practice,

practice
what we can learn from
a species, whereof
the habit is marked
out.

Relax

The women love each other
and the men love the women
and the men take part in each other
and the women don't.

The men are not all
homosexuals, and the women
are not all lesbians
but the women
are like the men, and the men
are very much like the women.

The cat wears bows, and the dog
wears rubber boots
The men
shit on newspapers, women
talk to animals
the children do the shopping.

The men love each other
the women go in circles
the cat is a eunuch
the children love the men
the women love the dogs.

The children are not all
homosexuals, the women
are not all
men. The dog
sits in a chair
smokes a pipe
and grows old.

Money

It is still in the use of money
(mysterious,
                    that good men spend)
as giving: in envelopes
in checks

in suits of clothes, which is the need of it
that goes beyond the groceries,

as much the twenty dollar
bill I'd put
away, and couldn't find.

To open up a book, and see
the money,

and go to sleep
and dream of money,

and wake up with a fist
and money
rising out of it.

Standard No. 1

There are hard things to say as
that we depend on each other
    are a couple of tots / you
make me feel so young.

It's all very goosey.
All the world loves
lovers & laughs at them.

Frightening. we'
r/*running across a meadow…*
and every time I see you grin…

That we do
so believe these things is
the end of sufficient action in ourselves.
Your
mother was sick: remember
    yr father cudn't
    eat hard food?

Well,
it comes down to the clothes
you've left laying around again.
And who the hell am I
strong Swede to be picking them up?

All the world loves
things that lovers do.

It's all very goosey & crazy &
hard to say: *I'm such*

a happy   in-
dividual.

Standard No. 2

Do we love each other beyond understanding?
Certainly.

Does the wise man shit in the forest?
Not when the ranger's around.

When the things you plan
    need a helping hand
        will I understand? All
the things you do
whenever you are blue?
Maybe.

    I'll be there, be
seeing you.

All the old romantic places
that this head of mine effaces,
    Always:

not
for just an hour
not for just a day
    for just a year, but
sometimes.

Jango

There is a wind that comes to mourn in these mountains
                              that hath the feel
        of a garment that hath the trail
        of wet gauze for your eyes
protection should your eyes
drop out
from the sight of Jango.

And the cloth flung
                    from her hip
is a mile wide/is the great   ruddy
ass of Jango
a mile wide.

        And she has tears for the Big Man
        flood for the buffalo incarnate
        itch for the scratch of hard muscle
        hung like the glaciers that carve
        in the creases of her skin
and how can she find him?

(It is not that I love hinder parts
that I see behinds crouched in this brush everywhere
        but loving what I see
of Jango.

I'm gonna sit in the crotch of a tree
in the crotch of these mountains
        and just
sit there/till she sends a quick doe women to love with—
to think   as we grind the hills apart—

Jango.

Merton

In Gethsemani, Kentucky
the jonquils stand in their own butter,
nothing in the air
in summer, in winter the snow always
already fallen.
                        This
infraction
of space, red rose, pink
roses (why
flowers at all?) those
delicate petals and stems.

Trees
Giant
Sequoia
tough
cactus, in Arizona
ganglia / yucca
growth
quiet in these hills
Kentucky
also, in August.

And in the city
carnations in the park, light
breeze off the river, summer
Chicago of jonquils
Roses on the avenue
the mad
stand of timber
in the garden of State Street.

Louisville—
Back in the world,

> *I felt like a man that had come down from the*
> *rare atmosphere of a very high mountain…*
> *but I found that everybody else was just getting*
> *up and having breakfast and going to work.*
> *And how strange it was to see people walking*
> *around as if they had something important to do,*
> *running after busses, reading newspapers,*
> *lighting cigarettes.*
> > *How futile all their haste…*

Back to Gethsemani
into the grain fields
hoed them
grew things
cut things down.
Then
came to things as beautiful
flowers standing in their own juices
a person in his own image
Christ, Christ's father
Poinsettia
Mandrake.

And this is the vision God gave me
was his house in Gethsemani
a host
of lilacs
burning on his altar.

And from the city they came into it thru barter
and I saw them come into it thru talking
then saw them come to it thru acid
into it thru passion, fire, limb & bark.

And I saw them come into his house singing
and I saw them come into it dealing
came into it thru brothers
into it thru a reaper,
a gleaner
to it thru a forked stick
divining.

Then Great Flowers was the vision God gave me,
a brain on a pillow on a hillside
a flowered heart in a chest,

and lung flowers
roses in cheeks, poppies
great root of Sequoia
lilies
in the tomb of a belly.

And this vision sent me back from his altar
(my Poinsettia my Mandrake) into this flesh
that grows in the wet fields
where all our saws
                    sang holy sonnets in the world of timber.

And thru this vision have I come to the moss door of the earth
having fasted and beaten my breast, having worked it
having sung it

and have come to the earth's door in pleasure
having lived off it
and close
to it—

        let me in
        let me in
in.

Super Bowl / 68

Lamonica reads the blitz and calls
the audible. On the line

there's Jordan & Kostelnik backed
by Robinson on the left.

Dixon
comes on the draw / he
gets by
                    Caffey.

There is an open field beyond
where he can see

F i l l e d / all at once

by Ray Nitschke.

Correspondence

April / 67

T. Olson,

I received your note.
I cant clean your windows.
Please get somebody else.

Your windows were not
cleaned since Sept. 28, 1965
and I cant clean them anymore.
I dont have the time, and I
dont care to clean them
when they are so dirty.
Please dont bother me anymore.
Thank you.

Yours truly
Tony

Dear Tony,

Let me start by saying, it is all true
and that my car even
is covered with dust, tho
I never wanted it.

I have to pass each day with
my eyes averted.
"Wash Me" it says
from across the trunk lid
& is so dirty.

But the windows dont have
such a voice. They stare
like I imagine Buddhas
being no longer transparent
and unobtrusive.

It is hard these days not
to want looking out
fearing the face of evil
disregard in my own skin.

Everywhere people are dying
tho they never
needed it. Women
becoming disgusted
with me and vice versa.

I have taken from September / 65
for that counsel & have seen you
daily, hanging from the sides of tall buildings
too far above to hear me.

Tony, it is time
I looked out for my windows,
accepted the pain
of that knowledge which is cleansing:
that sometimes there just
isn't anybody else.

Please let us come together in experiment
each taking his own side of the pane.
My windows and I are asking
to bother you just once more.

We promise to pay the extra fee.
"Wash me"

Face Work

"One's face… is a sacred thing, and the
expressive order required to sustain it
is therefore a ritual one." —Erving Goffman

The spider has no face,
    she spins her web
        in the corner of the basement window
a web like sac that hangs
and forms the cusp.
the fly
gives face, is caught, the spider walks
        along the web. The fly
is wrapped
        within each careful strand
the little spiders hang
above his head

And thru the web & grass
some legs appear.

The spider is a villain
the fly keeps
buzzing for an hour or more.

The lore
of giving face & names:
    each face
    is asymmetrical, each name
    so slightly
        incorrect,
as Horse
who came to rest
on a bed of tires,

they'd dragged him down the hill
with ropes,
then soaked with kerosene.

I still
remember what a face he had
and how the weather'd made it possible,

the hard-faced
Mexicans they'd hired,
who lit the rags
and threw them on the carcass

…who brought me face
as if a human signal fire
that drew the birds in closer,
smoke came forth from out his nostrils
& his eyes,
                & took him out of face
                into
a random photograph of nouns.

The sun breaks thru
the clouds. Across the strands
the spider moves,

there is a face-off in the yard
between my cat
& chipmunk, facing-up.

A dog
moves thru the web
to save his face. The cat
is given time

to say "excuse me," dog says
"certainly."

      The chipmunk
saves his head. The fly is dead
The spider walks
             along the web.

Tools

I am planning a job of carpentry; at least
I am thinking about doing it.

Sitting
in the back yard, in the evening—
the light fails, and I

think about my tools
and how I have hung them up:
professional.

The hammer is oiled against rust
it is very quiet
where it hangs

in the basement, beside the other tools
which are also quiet
they

don't touch each other. Carpenters
know about such things,
or any man

who can do such things
with grace. That's why
they only say: *let's get to work.*

I
talk about my tools, go down
even into the basement
to look at them.

I am no good at carpentry.

FISHING

Fishing

There is no graveyard I have found here yet
nor sought—
         middle of the narrow cape
the bay a haven now
the other side, the Sea
    its history of shipwreck.
    Nor are we
apart from that,
and in a dream last night did find himself
at edge of continent: a figure
waiting in a hallway
    shrouded, who was death,
and then was wakened to the light
from Highland Lighthouse flashing
on his wall.

I say
"himself" in order to avoid
specifics of a history,
    the graveyard I am looking for. The light
looks back upon itself; it sweeps
to inland in its turn
it crosses land
it wakes the dreamer from his dream.

America,
the nightmare in this placid zone
at edge of continent; he thinks
his dream prophetic
of his private life,
    but of your own—
    the shell of solitude
held to the ear,

only the Sea is heard, beyond
what masochistic hopes
are held by fishermen,
    today the bay half empty of its fish,
their nets that sieve out garbage
from the Sea.

What started here
began in shipwreck, nor could Thoreau
redeem it:
    measure the lighthouse, talk about
the quaintness of the people. There is
that mystery
of Sea that we perpetuate,
the land-locked
    quality of our lives. No one
will dispel it,
least of all the fishermen
deny that special understanding
we invest them with
in ignorance.

The Sea   The Light   The Pull
of moon is nothing
we can count on,
    think the shore still virginal;
our lives run inland
from that somehow tainted edge
of continent—

America: a house burned twice
in Bucksport, Maine, because
the fishermen disliked the architect,
the simple
    brutal power of the people here

at edge of Sea, the purest products
we believe as backbone,
rib of sand spit rising in the surf,
the very source
of moral fiber.

He celebrates himself, goes public
like successful stock,
believes the company he keeps
is bankrupt
          as the Sea is
owned not by the fish who live there
but the fishermen,
who come to dock in winter, cracking ice
from off their riggings, bundled against the cold
almost
          unrecognizable as human,
mysterious, as in his private dream.

What right to speak,
but that his grandfather fished
and took what human need he had
in bass and skillful casting of the fly,
the only real mastery
provided to his life
though lived it honestly.

     Croppies, bluegill
when the bass were gone,
the scratch of scales
against his palm,
the ever widening circle
of his lazy boat—

as in the lake in Oregon
he fishes with his brother, catching nothing,
thinking, somehow
    that's because he hasn't paid his dues
as fisherman: the care it takes
the touch
the time put in in waiting,
has not learned the patience
or the rules,
    but at his current age
lays claim, specific to his history.

They come against the pilings and the dock
at edge of continent
familiar
    to their moorings, smug
as if they held the secret
of the dream he had,
are like that shrouded figure
standing on their decks. He hears
the fish
        flopping in their holds,
the lines against the rigging
in the fog.
He knows that they are harmless;
in a way, he fears them.

    I fear them.

I fear my own specific age,
my aging, gray
hairs new in my beard,
    fear the dream's source
    the loss of power
    the empty ocean below my line,
garbage.

America,
who could stand on your shore
and not say these things?
deserted
of our families
our adolescence,
      who becomes less of a child
      too soon even at 35—

Grandfather,
I want that ridiculous gesture:
      your hand rests on my shoulder;
we are fishing
it is early morning
the flies stir in motes at the shore
our boat rocks in the gentle swells
      of our movements, we are
"horsing up" our gear
you speak
in a whisper, our lines uncoil
      perfect placement
in the air.

No graveyard then from where he sits
or houses burning,
      but the houses stud the hills like stone
around him;
none are open to him: guard dogs even here
and signs,
      as if a grave surrounded by a fence,
or in the hallway in the dream
the shrouded figure
beckoning
      himself to death, a final joining
of his human family;

but a nightmare
& he woke up screaming
warding off that figure
like a fish
    seems strangely magnetized
to movements of the pole, the line
invisible.

The gentle contract
that his grandfather had
    with fish he caught—
these fishermen
intent on business
    might as well use dynamite
as nets, or might as well
burn houses down
that stand against that retrogressive longing
for a past we think is perfect: America
where we have lived
    our adolescent lives out
    in a dream; this coast
this very edge of continent.
Thoreau, the beach still stretches out:
we dream we walk it in our sleep, a dream
    within a dream
within our disconnected spirits, body tossed
uprooted from our graves and lost
within a structure
    evident within the brutal business
    of the fishermen who count the fish they catch
as money—
    coin of bondage
    coin of business
coin specific
of America, we live on

and control ourselves
    the way their boats do
    over water,
and only slowly have we learned too late
the fish have left us here, alone
within a dream
of burned-out houses and of empty nets.

It all began in shipwreck, didn't end
in Bucksport, Maine.
The house was burning and the skillful
fire they'd set, they used again
exactly as the first—

    She walked among the townsfolk
    who politely nodded as she passed
    and didn't talk behind her back,
    nothing personal in their act;
they must have seen
her house as graveyard
of their magic lives
they thought as constant as the Sea
they used
    & used the fire
as much as fish are coin
to warn their lives away
from change.

At 35
he thinks American words
to hold himself within a similar fix,
the also retrogressive
longing for his grandfather's house,
the basement
    where they tied the flies

and coated them with wax;
they seemed
eternal in their casings—

fishing
is suspension of control we need
to come to them.
    We cannot understand them,
but to break the surface with explosives
or with nets, destroys
    the entrance we achieve
or hope to, with a filament of line,
a puncture
    in the surface of their element.
It needs respect and dignity,
that elegance of posture
    sitting quietly in the bobbing boat,
    the lure a kind of ritual
offering of control to them
(the line is not a trick
but measure of respectful distance needed
    from that real world)
the nature of our contract:
a filament
    intricate, with trust—

fishing is religion
if that means
connection to the Sea again
from which we came
that brought us to this edge
of continent, and warned us
with those brutal shipwrecks
off the shore.

Inland waters
where his grandfather fished
   (when I was young) were temples,
sanctuaries
of this Sea: that they allowed him
touch of fish
   and of his grandfather's human form
(he didn't know him well at all
    was not the point)
I was a child—

but fishing
has a quality unlike fire
that touched them coolly to the bone together,
and fish
   that surely can distinguish skill
would bite the lure his grandfather offered
(not his own).

Johnny,
you would hand your pole to me
so I could feel
   that sexual tugging on the line.
I didn't know you well at all—
   the line would race across the surface
of the lake.
We touched each other
intimate at those times.
I have forgotten how to feel such things.
There are no graveyards I have found here yet,
but this is what it means to seek them.

America,
there are those of us
   who never even reached

243

the outer beach Thoreau was walking on,
talking of the lighthouse
and the morals New England people have.

She speaks
of Bucksport, Maine, as if
the burning of her house were revelation
of her private life:

>   Divorce, when they had burned it
>   for the second time: "it wasn't meant
>   that we should live there."—

life with him already
going up in smoke.

She laughs, she is
    symbolic in her gesture,
    wants to walk among the friendly people,
    and the fishermen
        (her neighbors)
    nod to her and smile
    profoundly, in their common guilt.

>   It will not happen:

we have left it there
behind us
    at the water's edge.
And for himself
    has left it
somehow in the matrix of that lake
& gear & boat,
the way his grandfather managed
to unfold his line in air

and lay the fly
    in rushes at the shore:

it was
so irresistible
    the bass would seem
to simply come to lunch with him;
he'd merely guide them
swimming
    toward his boat.

And eating them
    their succulence
was almost
    sacramental.
He remembers how
it touched himself
specifically
    back to this continent again,
to life.

I say "we"
I say "himself"
    in order to avoid my part in this.

He sits
above the bay,
    can see
a single sailboat spar. The bay
is placid
      and the boat
as if at anchor rests
upon the surface of the Sea;

below it
    catfish, feeding on the bottom
ripping garbage with their teeth.

Between himself and boat
    a fisher-hawk is hovering in the air
dreamlike
in his constancy;

    he sits
upon the air above
the continent and Sea

              and then
he folds his wings together
then he dives,

pure in his anger
certain of his catch.

CITY

One

what is worthwhile
comes to us in song,
the City streets

the neighborhood
hood of street-lights
at day-break.

In this City
there is less room
now for music

my foolish heart,
Motown
& Chicago

laced with the same touch.
Our throats hurt
our eyes water

might as well
sing songs to enzymes.
Hudson

the Desplaines River,
the various colors at sunset
wipe your eyes.

Two

A land full of disaster
this year of election
a natural process

in which
the City remains safe
source of harm.

We have only ourselves to blame,
says the Bishop,
year of war.

Flood waters the east
but the City
remains calm

evening.
Even the moon is official,
source of light.

Three

these buildings, their
intricate patterns

against the sky   Let's
all go to the islands

it's like summer there
Puerto Rico

otherwise, the properties
of the City

slums, but
look at the flowers!

Asthma attacks, sun struck
on the streets of Harlem.

Intricate patterns, blocks
from the shores of the island.

Four

The nights still quiet
the streets

empty of crowds
at the still edge of the summer:

let that be the measure
of times long gone in the memory

I have not got
my own City a temple of sickness

returned too at the end of summer.
Somebody tells me stories

about those days I have not got
them, and their friends

holidays on the City's streets.
Forget it.

Five

Then too there are dances
elephant walks: women

in loose pants with tight thighs
could not play meaningfully

at a sport in such attire
this one & that.

The eye stops in cream
in ambergris

could not talk meaningfully
to a thigh

dances & songs
street of dreams.

Six

Splendor of discovered objects
against the senses

sense
of news and lost splendor

in them.
What is discovered fails

circle of lights and lights
moving on the West Side Highway

then circles the City
ring of bright jewels at a distance.

Now we are home
where the neck strains in the choker

a necklace of jewels
and false wealth at a distance.

Seven

The City opens her gates
her doors to the poor and lonely
then holds them down

until solstice, a comfort
of gone expectation in which
they can spend time.

The City teaches also
a lesson
to the unperturbed

that they can sit
firm, as the others live
in the midst of disaster.

Eight

In the City the ships go
to and fro,
with French sailors who

gawk at tall buildings,
with cargoes of oil
and heroin.

The connection
is always French never
Puerto Rican, African.

Georgia
Pacific Railroad bums
enter on foot.

The French sailors marvel
at the prices of trousers
and misunderstood food.

Would that all cargo
were human
or strange fruit.

Nine

but the City hath
built itself into columns
of steel, hath

hidden results
of machinery. In its walls:
rivets & lathed items.

One imagines
a glove stiffening
in concrete

from which a hand withdraws
its personality.

But a cornerstone
touch, of the Architect

in the hard edge
block letters, cut
with machinery.

Ten

as if a light were in them
had been turned out.
So beckon

only for wine. What else
but avoidance to touch them
who are not dwellers?

but the City
contains them, befouled
in its comfort of no interest.

who are drunk and vacant
like new immigrants: this
foreign place.

ELEVEN

Wanting to be public in a way
free of all strictures,
the City

is preventive. There is
a medicine we say we all need,
but it cloaks us

in resolve,
a coat of resolve,
a falseness

in which we parade commanding
our own space
and head down and closed. Blame

the City, blame
the tourists:
they've smiling faces.

Twelve

Blocks full of children.
the young teachers
bringing them back from museums

two by two. Building blocks,
cement sidewalks, they
reach a curb and gather.

Teachers
intense, inexperienced
in the company of children who are

inexperienced
in the ways of teachers, parents
the City itself: mid-town.

Black children, black
white & puerto rican teachers
all eyes and voices

correctives and attempts.
The light changes. Sad
blocks of empty buildings

behind them
dead, in the name of Power.

Thirteen

Aura of morning:
a false light

the City gives to things.
Our lives spent

in magic
hope of discovery.

Around this corner
Love & some old friends

assembled
News

we had thought profound
in that light

the buildings they stood for
and in front of

themselves are gone.
Now

magic of disappearance.
There is nothing there.

Fourteen

We walk close together
down the City's streets
our wrists are touching

occasionally
flesh against flesh

but the hard bones of the wrist
striking each other

against garments
or other people.

The whole thing
is inexplicable:
the City reminds us

that we love each other
and the world: the look
of the City's streets at sunrise

is a wonder. Our bones
hit against each other.

Isolate, in our safety.

Fifteen

The sea is calm tonight
the tide full

the moon lies
at a far distance

upon the river: Brooklyn
amazing & clean

in the rain seen
from the N train.

The Sea of Faith
Crane,

the train stops halfway across the bridge.
Struck dumb at the sight

so various, so beautiful, so new.
Ah

stupid:
a land of dreams.

HOME

1

Who makes of his wife a goddess, is subject
to certain depression
          thinks he's a king
or trash unworthy

to possess her even
live in the same house
with her.

          Either way her faults
pierce his groin like needles
also he walks around with a sick head.

Who loves her and then
seeks other women
faultless & perfect smelling
and longs for the nectar, he is trash
or a false king on his property.

He who loves her truly
however, will kiss a rash on her body
take in the smell of her breath in the morning—

          seeing her face in the textures of concrete walls
          in the bellies of other women
He discovers his real value
and finds his spot.

2

It could surely become more involved: we'd
say things about structure

the sexual possibilities
of every flat surface in the house

and the round surfaces also
and the pointed ones: all

the possible pleasures of invention.
There are new objects constantly:

this week
a table and a ches.

We walk out in our new coats:
we become more involved with each other.

3

How enter into it: as contract, I'll
do this you do that

thing: food on the table,
I'll move the car,

      we're
sometimes uncertain about the dishes, who
opens the bra-strap: discovery

constant discovery.

4

I cannot altogether formulate what I mean.
Our love is bondage or a migraine

headache we possess in common
        Slow poison of my stomach
I cannot for long eat food in another place.

And then too, you come, sideways
often at the wrong times into my life
        my thoughts
Agent

who would not like a fist fight
with someone he did not know.
You have to touch them
which is intimate.

5

Sometimes, when we have spoken,
you have carried those things with you,
however foolish: to work
in the lunch room—I have

        taken them too: the specific
touch of your body, whatever woman
I talk to, and you

are doing the same
with the men: we

enter the conversation
together.

6

Outside the wind is serious
that which enters
the cracked window
is tentative. We believe that
we have controlled something
tangible. in our lives, we say
we live in the eye
of a hurricane.
                    Down
bay-side, the wind is furious.
unaccountably: the ocean
is flat and calm: at the same time
in our lives, we say
hard things to one another: hate,
and then we love each other:
out, at the Cape's end
it comes together.

7

That which is tangible is a blessing
or does not enter as question:
          I'm sorry; will you accept that?
What kind of day did you have?

or else dinner and more talk.
And that's fine, too:
          each day, a new
illusion supplanted: information
vague information.

…Who loosens her bra
in the bright light of the bedroom:

aureole   .   aureole

8

Sometimes, we enter into things
in which we forget ourselves.
I mean, things done together

talking, or possibly
doing nothing tangible

times
simply sitting together
in your presence—

I mean
to say nothing here
of beauty
love, or any
thing we give a name to.
It is nothing tangible

but a sense of comfort
if we had to name it.

And that misses it
completely. When it happens

there is no one person
here, to name it.

9

Love—
that I have not spoken your name
and yet it comes to me
on the sand at Longnook   seeing
the boy walking
                    along the beach from P-Town. That
I should be doing this
one morning
                    early   before the sun
breaks on the forearm Leave you
in bed park at the lighthouse   then
go along that beach   no shells
or driftwood   only
that bright tower and light
behind me
            brings me
over the same ground   quicker
knowing
you are awake
await me
Miriam.

10

It is not that we think
            less of each other,
we expect too much
of ourselves, sometimes
wrong things

things fostered, those
coming forth thru passion,

memory, belief
                    in the way we feel
we live in the world

wrong-headed.

It is brutal: this week
how many times have I touched you?
I mean, passing
                    by you. Locked
in our own image
we think changing
tomorrow
            's thought of some new alteration
of passion, memory

rage at wanting to speak
and then be done with it.

The world changes
constantly
            and memory too
and yet
what is constant is distance, tho
that is what brought us together.
Miriam, there is no
depth of feeling in these words, but only

the lack of it.
                We become
the things we despise
because we are close enough
to hate them

       rage
in their constant distance
from us.

      Home
changes

it is brutal:
      the various houses shake
me, back into other places

of which I cannot feel
or talk about with sense,
and yet they have brought us together.

     —nor have you spoken to me
in a long time.

      I'm writing, you're
reading:
it is a condition of life
we live together.

It's not
that we think less of each other
or that it never happens

it seems
for a long time
I have not touched you,

nor have I touched myself.

11

Let me go on to say, as if
what was said before
had form
      and this
continued from it, say
I was 17 again
seeing you
and, what can I do with that?

Fact.
And then another fact: your hat
was bold, flamboyant
and your hair
      (and took it wrongly
when I said it).

Marie, it is
such wrenching of our lives
that does us good; to

see you once again
and then
to dream your paying the check,
the slight embarrassment
of gesture, as the time
      you talked about
the scar along your hip
at 17. At 33, you say
what can I do with that
and go
      back in my life again
renewed.

12

Nowhere a breath of scandal
        but in your mouth
remnants
        of a late dinner:
the meat rancid now
the wine turned to vinegar
and too many cigarettes.

In the morning we grew strange to each other
had touched only
        each other's imaginations
the night before.

How take these things as evidence
of our guilt: the dead meat in the air
sour wine on your breath
and I suppose mine also
was no picnic.

Upon leaving
our words were very sly
we did not touch each other all day.

Marcia,
we feared love and detection
counted the miles to Chicago
        dispersed there
and remained always
the alleged perpetrators.

13

The fact
occurring in some light
is the beauty of its existence.

It could be a light in the eyes,
as passage
            into another life:
those things
not left behind
unless, they are not spoken.

Or maybe the light in garments
a wife leaves around the house,
each specific gesture
seen in the light of her absence.

If I take you
into this poem
it is not casual:

in closed rooms, tho
some light present
we
    have looked at each other,

understand:
            fulfillment.
I am not speaking of messages;
occurrence
            whatever the light
is its own justice.

The rules
we get from the earth
        are simple:

behave yourself, do good deeds,
live in your body,
beware
that you love each other,
be honest about it.

Barbara: here in this room
writing this poem for you
I am somehow
warned, away from myself
into some different magnitude: it's Fall

the earth
lays waste,
            a ringed-necked pheasant
is passing out of the bushes.
The way
we say he ignores us
not thought
            as we understand it, but
his own life in the balance
(we call it) of nature.
He walks in a failing light.

What I am saying
is not matter
            of convention.
We both know people
throwing their lives away
on forms.

And I too
have probably done so.

That's why

I am not full of understanding,

or able to speak
clearly
        about what I think
of love.

A gentleman turns to a lady.
It is a matter of convention,
        earth
breaks open:

        Fall
the ringed-necked pheasant
is dead in his tracks
when the hunters come, tho
they walk in a different light
and are so clearly
awkward,

        as I am too
remembering
the light of your cow-eyes,
though they seem now
less domestic.

Do not think of psychology.
Is it so hard to accept?

It is.

Complications,
things blurred in a bright light
of occurrence,

a human light.

For me
the earth breaks open
again,
        a new pheasant,
in-
distinguishable,
comes out of the bushes,
and walks on the earth again.

The light softens
around his clarity.

14

The names of places and objects
the way the foot's spot
in the first snow
fills.

Disappearance of people
from memory: walking

in snowfall down
the hill from the High School,
Mary Lou:

name of a frame of reference
undone, as in *that place*
or *first kiss*

touch
of our own slim bodies
alone, in our rooms at night.

15

I remember your body it was dancing timber
smell of eucalyptus burning
the endangered house

          and stood apart in the woods together
in smoke, and revealed your breast to me
I was 9 years old.

Each
experiment with love starts

with a body on fire at a distance
          a woman always
standing in full length across the room.

Timber. The aureoles of your nipples
I could not touch

your skirt was moving in smoke
your ankles, covered with leaves.

16

Sometimes we are lost in the sadness
of our objects; how to extract ourselves?
          This chair, bought at a rummage sale
saliva, dry and holding the loom'd
evidence of greased heads of old ladies
dead now.

Or that I should want to buy
this coconut: face of a ring-eyed dog
carved into it, pathetic. At 25
          I slept in the still warm bed
          of a dead man.
I bought the bed.

Sometimes objects into the head in exuberance:
the lost smell of a part of the body found again
after many years. Salvage

because love too is often arrived at thru recovery:
this particular musky essence
I had forgotten

like the old romantic sound of a distant freight train
you too are arrived at
here, or somewhere in Utah
joined with a golden spike.

17

Fresh blossoms
            as if it weren't enough
            that you left this morning
and I discover them
alone, and can't give them a name.

It's Fall already
the blossoms seem new though,
yellow, possibly
Queen Anne's Lace? Or King Henry's
Venerable Crawler—
                        who knows
what evil lurks in a name?

The wind
is no longer warm
it goes *through* the weeds
and not over them as before,
            tho the sun's still bright.

Gone,
and so I have to write this lament
doubly for the two of us: myself yesterday
and the one who is here now
not knowing the names of flowers
foreign in his posture
bent down over them,
            a gesture of protest against
absence.

Who is it that shakes his head then
and stands up?
                    The flowers
yield to the fantasy
of a name: Rag Weed, moves
in the shared power
of the wind.

Miriam,
there are platitudes so deep
in the heart's core
we can't speak them,
            the way even I stand here
            is conditional,
call them
matters of biology:

flowers are brought up regardless
of names,
            hearts do
cleave to one another
beyond imagery. Brutal
& real, locked
in the same skin
is bondage.

And you are my twin,
converse of the face seen in these buds
complement into symmetry
light side of the shadow
            that falls over his shoulder now
the clouds closing—

it's Fall.
I walk toward the house leaving
            the history of that gesture:

the bent body, the look quizzical,
the strange buds—

and enter the door followed
only, by the first drops of rain.

18

Facts
become hard things to define.

I mean brute facts:
a knife when it cuts

the fact of love.
All these times

I have tried to get it said:
the cat pushing the mohair throw

brute fact
of a world full of resemblances

your eyes your
body

smell of your body:
cuts.

19

...said that I loved you, and that
is spoken again, recalled
of the different spaces in which
we are brought to this presence: it is
romantic
enough,
            high trees in the distance
the sky
            forming itself in its objects:
cloud cover, the wind, two
gulls over the water: distant
and yet closely, and yet...

we're the sum of our objects
of speech, each time
            we have said it
I love you: gulls

have appeared, the earth's moved
in whatever life, or place
into this present.

20 *(after Kelly)*

There is no history
but that which love gives
to a thing.
Sleeping
            it is your hand
I touch (my own?)
I cannot tell.

I am asleep
then wake as in the joke
what is that? your absence
I have touched
its history.

       It goes to sleep.

21

Last summer, we put in many hours
of work around the house.
The other night
     with friends, we talked
of all the work we'd done
and other things.

Such
     sad simplicity
of time, that splits the distance. You
were sitting on the couch,
      our friends were there

and gathered
in the matrix
of our talk
     a distance
from the things we said
and from each other

yes
in time, but also
in the spaces of the room itself:
the smoke that made it tangible.

How hard a thing, and seldom
        that our faces
make an imprint, other
than in air. Your hair
keeps growing longer.
What could I expect?
but that last summer
takes its measurement in hair:
the length of it you carry
in a changing way, a different
tilting of your head
your hand
        that brushes
        hair away from face.

And of our friends, their talk.
And of myself

who's carried back these days
        to funerals.

Or of another friend
who finds it hard to eat:

that I can see such action in his face,
that is his own,
                but takes me back
into my life: my father's
inability to eat
…and saw his death prefigured
in his actual face.

The sad
simplicity of time
we fill with gesturing

and sex. The hair
grows natural and like
a forest
      or a tumor, is
a kind of clock, and yet the words
we think
      can form a closure
as in sutures
of the skull, or make a fusion
as the smoke does
standing
in the air
      that only separates,
defines the time as distance.

And of these words I speak
I'd form a matrix or a web

…but not a web, no
metaphor
      or image: but an action
so to fix my friends and you
in time.

      I do not mean this poem.
I mean an insult or a real whip.

We are our faces, certainly.

we face each other
when we talk
      we love
to put our faces close together.
Saving face
or facing things

that happen
        or another face, that we
should think our faces sacred things,
we cover
        or reveal
ourselves. we sit in circles, so
to see the faces
        of our friends, and yet,
at times, the face is drained,
turned inward
        into space and time: we make a face
to hide it.

My father's form was rocking
in the chair.
He was so thin and light
        the chair
would barely move,
        his eyes would rock, and I
would find that I was rocking too,

our friend
who finds it hard to eat
was rocking also
on the phone last night;

his face is turned to distance
we can't enter
                though we try
to form a web
or matrix.

The night before
that call: our friends were here.
we talked of all the work we'd done,

and other things.
It was no more than this:
we spent a simple night together.

I've been
only speaking for myself.

22

It is not that I come at the food
            out of embarrassment
nor slide up to the table
whistling—O

the seriousness of the matter: hunger
dross of the weight of gold in the mouth,
dead things.

And of all this old tales are told,
the starving king, the robber—
bridegroom & cannibal.

            And yet
we hunger for that which lives: a body
at rest or on fire
the constant changing circle of lips.

This food, I approach with grace
even passed in a doorway:

            your breasts
inverted cups of wine
the tight ring of your anus,

my mouth waters.

23

The gulls come farther inland when it rains
as if the Sea itself
        in its deposits on the land
were there. They drop
and swoop to fish in the longer grass
            then bank
        and rise up puzzled before they hit
then move away
till they get high enough to see
the final demarcation of the land,
then drift
        then hold themselves
in that location

                /

My heart's in the highlands too sometimes
my body also turned
                    to whatever job or pleasure,
        the mind gets lost
dips, and returns again
to you: my. Sea of Tranquil Waters.

                /

Always
driving past the dump
we see gulls lining the largest hills,
a string of pearls like wisdom
        half way between
the garbage and the sea.

24

It is that we spend time with people
we don't know
          approach the elegance
of the dance there
with them:
copy of bird's trip in the bushes
hawk's dive / our paradigm.

I sit in my brother's house and say nothing
to him. fishing for trout in the high lake
we don't catch them, watch
the dance of the Osprey
          and Crane.

Love's
lost in the synapse of biography
fake lives we believe we have lived together.
We are in no way like these birds

we watch them, they
dance at the end of our eyes

they hate each other
now, here in their fight
          in their flight
they do not spend time with people.
We don't know them.

Later
we drink beer and argue
abstractions. the night
closes on my brother's house / home

to him, my home
       across the continent.

Miriam
it is only the dance of love
& the dance of hate
immediate we can live with.
Center, of elegance.

The birds migrate.

25

Whatever goes on with us is extendable:
the rights of man
and not as a crow flies,

    the gull's body in air
fluctuates. The state of The Nation
is measured in The Nation's garbage.

My brother talks of the City
as if he'd been there:
      men on the lookout for money only,
Depraved Seat of Power.

A man in Detroit
vacuums the City's sewers: diamonds
false teeth, a string of pearls

     identification
bracelet of fence
where the crows sit.

At the end of sight
the gull's body
     floats on a solid object
        which is the air.

My brother talks of the cities he's been to.
I kiss your legs & knees in the City.
Whatever goes on with us is extendable.

My brother talks of a fictional city,
without you.

26

The woman who comes carrying flowers
     toward me, sun in her eyes, that
romantic attachment
to what might have been
what is
flowers torn from the ground or cut
her arms dying around them
and mine, work scabs
     on the backs of my hands
waiting her arrival
and solstice.
She places them into vases in the house
where they too shall thrive.
You sanctify each day.

27

That each poem written derives from love
or works in defending against it
that it is, therefore
          not loving itself
but talk

about such properties
we name:
          bright double aureole
of breast, names of the tools we use.
Our father's names, the tender list
of family resemblances

against which things act, defend
ourselves thru talking.

In that arrogance
my love, I had wanted to say such
delicate, sweet things to you
derived from death
or from that talk of freedom:
that we are free to choose, at least

some life within our heads,
can love those things
we choose.

          But I meant straight
from human love, and even that
specific. Freedom
is a nonsense word
if everyone is free

to love each thing
we touch, or talk about.

So I am tentative
and wrong
                to say each poem derives
but even at its best
can only speak
            these words
that have no other life.

                        *

Thru this dirty window now
the handy-man
works on the water tower
cat
        moves thru the space between us
        focuses
the eyes against
the place she moves:
past brick
                in spaces

she is thought to own, until

the wrench he uses
clicks against a stanchion
and she's lost
            as much
a fluttering of cloth
that was a woman's bathrobe
only after
she was moving (cat or woman)
past another window.

*

Remember
you can tell when I am angry
sawing in the basement
                    hear it
in the changing rhythm
of the saw itself.

The saw was bending
worked against
the motion of my arm.
I was an inch away

you heard the counter
energy, the thought
that I could force it thru,
and did
            but cracked the board
against the grain.

You are like that board to me
your weapon, also, silence

I could break you too.
Your wrist is thin
you have no strength to speak of.

And even that's the same: the structure
in my mind,
            I'll use this last good board
to finish up the tool-rack.
Both of you are objects
I would use.

Words
too are boards, and if that's true
are nonsense terms
if everything is board-like

as is Freedom, Love, whatever
magnitude
I use
to bracket in my life—
my way of
facing objects, therefore
structuring my face.

That this derives from arrogance,
that nonsense words
avoid
      their honest derivations:

that we could give our language
force of root
and be that root, we name
      twist it
till it is ourselves, un-
recognizable: *is that a root?*
It was, but now
no more than use we make of it
and even that
no action—
only talk.

          *

No wonder it is hard
to speak of love
and foolish.

I'm not finished yet.

*

Another time: we'd
talked of sex as power
and a friend of ours seemed nervous
at the thought that he'd
not thought of that
before, as literal
taking of his wife
        who is another friend,
whose hair
is longer now. A power
keeps my eyes upon her
getting used
to changes in her aspect,
I keep looking to possess
the way she slips away
as distance,
            power
to hold her while she changes,
should she loose her place
as object. Like a board
is sawed and painted
lost within the structure
of the house.

Sex is power then
as much
as Love is Freedom
which is nothing that exists
outside ourselves, our
private, foolish world

resembles like another metaphor:
a mirror or a circle
always back
        to keep that sacred face
together

and yet another time:
when I had tried to face
a house I'd lived in, they
     had torn it down
replaced it
with another house, could see
     as aura of the first
the way the pipes had frozen:
winter of my father's death,
in summer
     we had painted, seemed to make
it larger, changed
its very structure. And the garter snakes
below the porch, my sister's accident,
the beer caps falling
from my pocket, time in jail,
street fights
getting drunk
off beer,
     the time
my mother used
that silence on me

for a week
     we didn't talk:
the strongest presence
I remember of that time.

Not a single evidence
remains of it, they've
graded

but I take that house,
as converse of the facts I know,
possess it.

That of objects—
that of love—
that of possession—
that of family—
that of a useless speech—
that of the saw—
that of brackets—
that of a single
        existent thing.

        I have finished now.

but first:

        that properties of wood
are somehow constant,
that I broke the board
thru rage—well,

it was silent. Neither
did it give me time
to think about its grain and texture.

I could have loved it then,
if loving boards is possible: *the word*
is what I mean to talk about—
like Freedom, Love

or any
     foolish magnitude

(it slips away) and we
keep talking
       til
there's nothing more to say

defend
     against the silence,

Miriam.

Another word.

I do not say it.

Where you sat,
your body's indentation in the chair,

was not your absence
     but that fact itself,
to use in foolish poems.

and yet remains
itself, as silent as the board.

28

The delicate beauty of our friends' wives
at sundown. Everybody
     loves adultery. They gather
around me in their passion
they await my embrace, news

of an alternate life
banal acts of a kind of incest.

I love
women who stay at home
        but want to leave it.
Touched into shame
I take them each to my chest
at sundown, when they are cooking
and I am waiting
for your return.

29

Simply, the oblique passage
        of your body by my chair:
you show me a face walking toward me
another one, walking away

disgusted
with everything at this moment
        your hips cannot express it
that variety of statement
impossible.

        honey in the swollen fruit
        ambergris in the wound
I take this seriously.

30 *(after Ovid)*

Lovers find it delicious
to fuck in the daytime

if they love each other purely
are not prone to dark imaginings
pretense of other women
or men. I wait

'til light enters the closed blinds
as if a wood outside at twilight
or early morning, its branches
modest intricate patterns
on the bedspread and the wall

beside the door you'll enter
as yourself. I know
that gown a hundred times at least
your hair, untied and familiar
halted pacing in your modesty

you come. Not the first wife
or any lover, real
or imagined is specific
to you: explosion of fantasy
except the true maiden you are.

That game wherein I lay
waiting tempter, ravisher
homebody, husband.

I pull your gown away. No need
to itemize. Partly undressed
in woods in faint light

virgin, goddess
wife.

31

This one is awkward, because
it is written in need: the earth breaks
open, painful, trees come
into existence.

It is all simple
it happens—this
does not happen
is written

abstracted—possibly
the head breaks
too:

        the first wife
Crab-Woman   Beautiful
Cripple.

This is addressed to…
need:
to have said *get a cane!* Can't
drive a shift car
I had one.

        Crutch
for the crab, walking
whatever vector. I'm

not a simple man
this is awkward, painful
to say it: the earth breaks—

the head breaks open.

This is addressed to

    Annie Crab-Wife
Beautiful-Cripple,

and Miriam
we live here—
make plans.

32

Love brings me down in the morning
then brings me up:
your feet
    at the bed's edge
particular hang of the ankle
the simple
fact of recurrence.

But in the light breeze
    (salt off the bay
      crystals in soft air)
another room

and woman
her feet absent
her small tennis shoes
in morning's sad light
    in the back of the closet
after she'd gone that time,
brings me down.

She must have stood in the closet half dressed
then quick and impetuous
ran right out of her shoes.

I did too.

Your feet shoeless
        pigeon-toed
dimpled by first light
soft as the salt air, sheer
cleanness of your step
insouciant, brings me
back up again.

Trail of phosphorus
walk of the pigeon
I follow across the rug.

33

A remembrance of things said
in time:
        Annie, a small joke
hand covering your nostril's flare
in embarrassment
you laugh. I

too, fearing my body left you
a bag of worms, pig memories
vanity.

        Quick to discover
after two years of marriage
lust, we

fucked and left each other
touchstone of specific temperature.
Who could stand that close
and not be weary? Without love
we raged in each other
fell apart
        in perfect exhaustion
we even talked a little. It is all

old-fashioned: solution of groin
impossible.

I think of your body often.
I don't think about you.

34

Always the unexpected
passage of things in the common air
spice of life
        a lock of my own hair falling
down my vision, grey strands
I grow older.

You enter the room carrying tea
the unexpected
        cinnamon when I taste it.
Each year the passage of news into my life
and variety, you bring me
what is mine.

35 *(the dead)*

The nearness of you
        tho you've gone to work
and I'm alone in these four rooms
is evidenced
in your blouse lying across the chair
the placement of ashtrays & books, even
        the flat cool breeze sliding
under the half-cracked window
at my side.
                Outside
snow general all over the terrace
in its drifts, the brick
wall around it and the metal railing
snow capped. Paul's
        too real picture & yours
where my eyes go
to the wall.

Nearness
of friends dead and friends
gone to work
        in your new dress
and boots (old boots
in the closet)
        a pair
left in our house on the Cape
where the snow also is general
        poles marking the land
        standing in drifts.

Reluctant to start
a movement in real time,
fixed line

of a row of trees, a man
stands in them as vector
or gesture of open
coat, wind down boulevards
        a row of low buildings
passed on a Triumph
in West Los Angeles
Pasadena. Annie
sleeping together
        waking
together, in boredom, in real time.

The mind goes in its junk
to the wall: camera
and man standing
under a snow bridge
in the middle of gesture,
his nearness.
It is not himself. Not
        that a camera lies,
the eyes
go to the wall—

        was of stone & blank face
Sarah
        holding the rope, Paul
hanging below
both
watching the camera
        goofing. Hat
cocked on his head
blind light in his glasses. Serious
Sarah.

The mind throws out junk
objects
        gather in their places
ashtrays & books, your blouse
the nearness of you.
The mind's
junk is a history of women
in pictures
all those things done wrongly.
We live wrongly. But
that we live in these things,
go to the wall—

        was of stone
        like a carved plaque
        of the war dead, hand holes
        of the names in the letters
                grave stone
        worn in the weather
        sight extension of my father's life
                standing
        in his body in the general snow.
        He is 59 now.
        click.

How then to extract myself
from these dead
        "How rare, the move to center
                where we live":
the nearness of you.

To be home free of the mind's junk
is a history of bondage
        pictures

of women loved wrongly
and men.

Go to the wall then
there is nothing there
        but flagellant
but stone's message to stone
vague scent of bodies in bed or on fire

impossible elegance flesh has
retreating from muscle and bone,
        a short distance
so much bulk
a bundle of sticks
the loved corpse
technician.

                    *

The chair sits in the room's center
it is free of the wall
around it
are fixed objects: books
and the made bed,
a shell on the table beside it
        In each case the agreement
was contractual, "you
stay, I'll go."
Sun
makes the chair beautiful
sunlight enters the shell
all these things are particular
it is a lovely chair. the shell
is made ridiculous by the light
It is ourselves we love.

*

I want constancy.
I want to live on in the face of death
        in the face of those dead.
I want my father.
I want my fingers
        gathered in the letters on the stone.
Want your body, your objects
this fixed roof.

The wall before me
        is empty
beside these closed frames of photographs
isolate.
        Faces of times that are dead now
        (you were a child then)
outside
snow constant in drifts in the starlight

the nearness of you: Home
ceases to vibrate.

It's not the pale moon that excites me

you return
as the same one
who left me.

36

I had wanted to tell you something
about our lives
and what we do together:

a large thing
I have forgotten

many times
I have learned it again:

it is a lesson therefore
the times are hard.
Sometimes

when we are together
I feel I could write you a letter about its
lacking necessity

in what is already
complete. I

would like to tell you about it.
I have forgotten
what is was.

DOCTOR MIRIAM

Priorities

'You have to take things as they come'
is a worn currency;
    depending upon your mood:
an answer to fear of age
or alcohol.

2 o'clock
is maybe the worst part of the day:
    means you got thru half of it
but still have a way to go.

Today
before you left for work
you came to me where I was working,
looking for scotch tape,
    and then you lifted and turned your dress
and fixed the hem with it.
                       Temporary
desire raging
even in morning's look above your knee:
I take it as it comes
and almost as important—
such simple ingenuity.

I had a wife, once
would tape her spit curls to her cheeks:
    she had a troubled need
to have her hair done
carefully.

That makeshift hem will hold for a little while,
and that's enough.
I do not want to make too much of this.

It's only that the day began with lust
and some discovery,
and that your hem's sufficient.

A Note

I thought today it would not rain
and it didn't
    and I was right again.
Clouds
all day long, opened and closed
with a certain symmetry
    letting the light in
and that too is accurate.

Sometimes, I'm so certain about
such things that it seems
the future
    is predictable. You called
5 minutes ago, said you would be late,
and I'm going out.

What I wanted to tell you is that
the sun made that circuit you spoke of
around the apartment, in a pace
    that today the clouds changed
into a kind of cuckoo clock:
each room, at odd hours, lit up.

    I was wrong again:
there'll be no one to tell that to.
I'm going out soon.

Ok.

I've hard boiled an egg for you.
It's in the refrigerator. the one
with the face on it.

Now you are smiling
And I am right again.

Tree

Thought I'd cut that tree down
 'cause it blocked my view.
(A bush really, a pattern
of stripped twigs of a sort
something
   like a spread hand held
before the face
with thin fingers.)

And cut the grass down first
with a borrowed power mower
 you ride on in a circle
claiming the lawn back
till the tree seemed larger where it stood,
then trimmed it down to its lower branches.

Now
we sit in the yard and drink
our booze and unobstructed view: the house
at the water's edge,
the Sea
 folding upon itself
seems closer now
   the slope
the yard makes hard to gauge,
where it drops off.

   It is
a simple loss of reference that we see,
a thing grown larger in its absence

like those things
we say we have, and never
touch or realize: a lamp,
a casual friend, a window frame,
a dead friend, a father exorcised,
    the way
you find a bathroom in the dark,
books & a life of shame,
                              all
such vague and useless things,
but they keep our world straight.

The yard may open perfect now
and yet when I look out I see

    that real & sad expression
on your face
I saw first when I cut it down

and carried it
like some delicate antler trophy
past your face
    sad and transparent
through the moving branches seen—

always
a point of reference.

Cotton Wood

It's a lazy day—

and that means the heartbeat's sluggish
or with its stream. Or more simply
just that it rained last night,
the roof held, and we've
    released that impending anxiety
against leaks and the placing of pans. And how
explain such things further?

                2 doves sit
in short grass, and peck.
Above them the wind blows
too furiously for us
to get out and do things in it
and so we sit.

We read. And after a while
the pages themselves seem to relax
    under our fingertips, the light comes
again, the wind quieter now
and less heavy.

    We can see better.
We turn the lights off and begin
to think about doing things, and then

    it starts to rain again,
we settle back in.

    How make a pretense of life
    as a permanence? it passes, is

as any mood
        returns in odd cycles,

like the Cotton Wood
stood that day for us, in its menses
only in passing:
                the bits of its aura,
some found after in our clothing.
You
were not there then.

It was somebody else I was with, you
were probably with somebody else too.
It was a lazy day.

    Look:
    now there are 5 doves.
Lazy. You read a book. I continue to sit
get up
    go out and paint the house trim a little.
It starts to rain again.
It seems to continue.

I remember the way the white
bits came quite literally cotton floating
        obliquely sideways
to the road, traveling
almost horizontal to the jeep
we were in
and the green tight packed forest
of aspen.

        Then
we were passing by it, one
white tree shedding

its cotton & seed.
We stopped the jeep
        bits of cotton wood lodged
in our clothing and hair.
It was somebody else I was with then.

        The rain stops again. The doves
        turn in a half-arc
                and land
        in the same place again.

        There are 4 now.

There were two of us—
        (so full of ourselves
we could hardly wait to get back—)

and made love, it seems now, so totally
even our clothes
                        stirred in their places
on chair, bed and floor,
came up
in that breeze

our moving bodies made
tossed out
        their seeds also
from skirt folds and cuffs:
cotton wood fluffs
flooding the currents of the room.

It was a lazy day.

You read a book. I continue to sit.
It rains again

but the sun bites thru in places, enough
to send shafts of dust motes or seed drifts
in at the window,
and light
falls over your shoulder now
Here
where we both are.

For a moment
your body framed in the window seems
a construction of incredible permanence.

     I would call it
     'this woman reading'

till I see
your eyes over my head
on the blank white wall:

you are not reading at all—
were probably with somebody else too.

It's a lazy day.

Messing Around with Patterns:
English & American
For William Dalzell

The coffee is turned down low, sputters
and seems to have
   irregular false starts in the kitchen
no rhythm like a metronome.
It'd drive you crazy trying to play
tho a simple kind of song it makes
after 40 beats or so
it's entirely possible there is a pattern
after all.

     The sun
late, because of daylight savings & the energy crisis
nevertheless rises,
   sheets against these dirty windows closing
much of the light out.

I put
grain on the terrace
3 jays come and ignore it, form
the living points of a triangle
spaced out, on the superstructure of the water tower:
blue jays grey with soot.

First day of spring (rain), attend
in the interstices
   a jet trail in high cloud cover.
The jet itself emerges
turns in a bank in its landing pattern
close to a jay's body.

The breasty
clouds clutch the plane between them,
    then melt and fade away.

The coffee fails
& then picks up its beat.

What is revealed?

Oddness, order
and a care for order. The architect
Lightfoot built Claydon House, cut up
and unassuming from the outside
but formal.
And inside, possibly
the most beautifully reasoned staircase
in the 18th Century
    (given the Chinese influence
      given the Gothick, spelt with a 'k').

The carved wood
of the picture frames, the massive
airy shrine like structure with its empty niche.
    Bangles
sputter in the railing's fretwork
at every step,
           across
inlay
of mother of pearl, of ivory.

Opulence
at cost of grinding the poor. Yes,
but Capability
planted a million seedling trees
for one landscape, that would

not be realized for 4 generations
at a large cost: so
a weird opulence (+) a weirder surety.

Here,
grey jays rise a little and shift
on the black metal. Sky is blue now
in the new triangle. Jet
is pinned there in its turn
    in the middle of centuries
of technology.
              The breasty
clouds spread & melt unnaturally,
and beyond that…

"But the Solar System!" I protested.
"What the deuce is it to me?" he interrupted impatiently:
"you say that we go round the sun. If we
    went round the moon
it would not make a pennyworth of difference
to me or to my work."
              That's Sherlock Holmes, a different
kind of capability (end of the 19th Century.)

Here, back in the 20th again,
    I've left the apartment—
been to a lecture on English Houses—and I'm
walking Lexington Avenue eating macadamia nuts

thinking: earlier, passing
among rich brownstones in the East 60s,
    how the dogs came out in complex patterns
in the mist. Plots of grass
squares planted
& small trees cupped in wire

in the planned concrete, and signs:
curb your dog, but they
come out like a symphony:

an afghan
shits at a tree's base
a poodle raises a leg against
somebody's Mercedes. There's a lot of talk
and compliments about breed. A boxer farts discreetly.
They all smell & mark their territories,
a few scowl and yap at encroachment,
there's an evident morning tryst or two.
The owners wear
the skins of dead animals on their backs.
various piles of shit steam in the morning mist,
the street is ripe with plans
    the City Fathers obviously understand.

These are the City Fathers,
who walk their dogs and go
out to their country houses
    and plan formal gardens
and turn the City to ruin.

A street
in London in the 18th Century
was a planned affair, a sense of community
shattered here in the 20th:
it's territory these dogs seek
    who live so close together
are driven insane
by crossed and broken patterns.

In the 19th
it was Pitt Street,

workers tenements under a bridge
in the literal shadow of Westminster Abbey.
　　"This, Sir, is capable
　　of becoming a fine landscape":
is how Brown got his name, and made drawings
and planted seeds and saplings, changed
　　　　a river even
into a lake. And now
4 generations later
the whole place has grown
very much the way he drew it: *that's*
Capability,
a lesson to city planners:
　　a weird opulence, surely, but
a weirder, realized surety.

The dogs shit
in the morning mist
　　which is in my mind now
back on Lexington Avenue with my nuts, heading south
in the afternoon. I find—

a maverick arc light/burns in the day light
at the corner of 61st Street, brighter
even than sun is
　　on the bright side
of the avenue.
It helps the sun fire the street.
The rest are dark and blind eyed
and reasonable,
　　　　　　　　until
clouds cover the street for a while
and that lone foolish light,
　　in place of the solar system,
spots the corner.

When the rest come on at 7
the maverick
'll burn no brighter:
could not pick it out in a crowd.
 The City has it:
 it needs repair, but I
watch it
and think of another maverick:

   Sherlock Holmes—his limits

1. Knowledge of Literature.—Nil.
2.   "   " Philosophy.—Nil.
3.   "   " Astronomy.—Nil.
4.   "   " Politics.—Feeble.
5.   "   " Botany.—Variable.

 . . . .

 Knows nothing of practical gardening.

6. Knowledge of Geology. Practical, but limited. [but]

 . . . .

 He appears to know every detail of every horror
 perpetrated in the century. [and]

 . . . .

12. Has a good practical knowledge of British law.

 . . . .

     but
certainly came too late for us, e.g.
Ruskin: "Ornament applied to building = Architecture."
(or) "If it doesn't naturally move, carve it."

 Although
in Scott's study,
where he wrote *Waverley* & created 'Gothic', there's
Blake's Canterbury Pilgrims on the wall,

and that's a maverick vortex (–)
a balanced capability.

Jays & plane,
the coffee-sputters,
     and half-mad shitting dogs begin to fade.
I've got
only maverick lights in my head
and a half-gone bag of nuts.

                    I offer
"They're cheaper and better across the street"
to the young woman wanting
macadamia nuts, in the gourmet food shop
in Bloomingdales,
     who smiles
and says they're for her boss's wife
and cost isn't the issue.

Blond like me, certainly
not from New York either:
     a capable enough mid-western girl,

whose breasts sputter
at every step
bouncing the bangles that she wears
over the tooled fretwork,
and do not fade or melt.

                    The eye
is allowed to stop in cream:
no energy crisis there.
and Sherlock
might have attended that
     tho a little

too analytically. The whole history
of the mid-west
        is in her eyes,
where pigs are snuffling still,
there, without care for territory.

I want
to *hold* those breasts
but cannot
        make the move fast enough
with her, where

we'd head into the past of
our dumb American surety:

  sock-hops
  the back seats of cars
  fretting with bra's latch
only
to somehow cure
this present pain. The future
is totally out of the question.
        no tangible leavings.

The natural
beauty of the American countryside, the sad
unplanned ruins of
  the elms cut down to allow
houses that are very pragmatic to go up.
A short view of things
about as far away
        as her breasts are,
and shall remain.

Well,
    she has fine teeth in her smile
like the measured interior of Claydon House,
two cubes forming the great hall
in no way natural.

    She's a maverick tho
as Flo was
and the little pseudo Chinese dwarf-like Buddha God, who sits
on a pedestal on the floor below
the niche they took him from
to clean it up,
              and found
he would not fit back again
without they'd possibly
break Lightfoot's carvings up,
who had
Florence Nightingale
    in his foresight,
who lived in Claydon House and put
paintings of dour nurses in those
lovely reasoned frames.

    She gets her nuts
    and leaves, and I

wonder did I turn the coffee off?
is the pot burned?
what am I doing out here?
shopping, I have bought nothing. The clouds
come again
it starts to rain. I imagine

the jays shifting on the slick steel
maintain the shape.

The plane is gone
the damp grain moving unnaturally,
punched & turned by wind,
little grains roll & move:

mavericks all,
but thru that a form attending
hardly worth the effort
defining
    points in a matrix.

A highly confirmed empirical science
mathematics is not
nor geometry
    nor architecture, save
in the use of it
as a surety:

    attend
Lightfoot, Capability, Florence Nightingale (not jays
or 19th Century magpies bringing
all things bright & glittery to prevent
a niche where the eye can rest), the un-
natural beauty of the English countryside
in which we
    with our limited foresight
cannot dwell:

    opulence (+) surety (−)
the natural beauty of the American countryside
we have not got
    much left of a quality of regard for (−)
enthusiasm (+)
a fucked up concern for technology: a most
highly confirmed empirical

science of short-sighted pragmatic nonsense (+)
a total lack of attending (–)
the mad Lightfoot
    and Capability holding
4 generations of seed money.

Like a Mayday, it seems
the end of winter's near. I hear
the grey jays'
    identifiable squawks
still in my head,

a paradigm
    that turns them back to blue:
a total, half-assed
locked in the present
American capability,
    a shunt of attention.

I'm home again.
The burnt coffee is close to oil
    (I taste it with my finger.)

The jays are gone. The cat
sits at the window watching
the empty tower,
    the fled niche.

In the box of grain
thistle has begun to grow
already, in the turn of one day
    (I attend the few green shoots.)

There is no pattern.

But for the cat begins
a certain garden
on which she has designs.

AESTHETICS

1

Paint what you see
is already a philosophical problem:

a blood-spot on the eye's membrane
absent in the still-life.

Still
life goes on, possibly
somebody buys the painting
who is slightly blind.

And how can we agree on beauty
even in women these days?

What you see is what you get.

The student asks: just how
does reading Joyce relate to my life?

& answer: it is *in* your life.

2

as if all these things
were part of memory

that we invented: a passionate
existence for ourselves,

a fantasy
of great glory.

Speak of the fine name
Anzio & Citadel,

all very hazy
as if seen thru X-ray

or on a silver screen.
Invented

in all its loveliness
in all its cool distance

& magic.
Bones and the shadows of flesh

on the X-ray
our sweet History.

3

I still remember the shape of Doyle's pot
Weed Pot and half golden
like a paradigm
she held in her hand.
Then

took us to her place
to see her craft, she said

and had grown flowers
and a multitude of good weeds
lining the drive.

A woman of obvious passion
opened the garage door to us,

hundreds of misshapen objects
she called pots:

plenty of imagination
pure ugliness.

4

Take the animal, always
in its insouciance

down a path of glory
we say we lust for

that place of heart
where only passage

defines us.
Sylvia

talks of the young boy
brain-damaged & foul

who finally recognizes
himself on the videotape,

that's me, he says.
Take the cat

not knowing itself in the mirror,
is it better?

5 *(for T. W.)*

What is white
in me is not like black
is not enuf
to say   bewilderment,
the cause of death the same.

And understand
I'm speaking of myself.
respect the body's temple
as a thing
impossible to enter, or

I put my tongue inside a poison heart.
The operation is successful:
both of us are dead.

6

the theme runs counter to the plot
the whole lacks unity

the symbol
of the great church as a castle

as a phallus
as a mythic device

is weak
when it rains it stands for death

the butterflies
however, stand for life

the crack of the tree's twig
in the night wood

is obvious

success
depends upon the acting.

7

Trees in the distance
given the name

and we find ourselves
believing in explanation

as the real world.
Cause & effect

are properties of language.
The trees beckon us

across that distance
and into shade.

The name framed in our minds
we do not enter,

but forest.

8

My friends make judgments about others,
those known in the flesh or otherwise
intimately, thru some art.

They have given us
too little of themselves,
they say.   They say
  this poem is dumb
  X has a broomstick up her ass
  Y is an academic.

They have given us
a little of themselves is why
we know them well enough
to talk.

Z enters the room.

I bless my friends
who know a little
of the grace of silence.

9

The language being the same thing
I speak here of Ethics: one man
in a tom coat
one resplendent in Mink.

'what the rich can afford to buy
is better' is a fact:

the dense meat of the rooster
more succulent than the hen.

The rich would have us believe
in our own myth of their decadence,

the soothing lie.
The feel of Mink is exquisite,

the seats of the Rolls Royce
conform to the owner's spine,

you live longer.

10

The subject was boats or roses
or the State of the Nation's
     Capitol on a windy day.
Say
it was a finer thing
like the Rights of Women
or a casket of ambergris.

Whatever
'…we cannot think, we cannot think: we cannot
therefore say what we cannot think.'

The Rose Bud opens in a Freudian manner:
names we have taken to hide in,
the perceptual solipsists
we all are.

The paired butterflies are already yellow with August
Over the grass in the West garden.

The woman's eye is the eye of the man focused,
'…thereof one must be silent.'

Talk of the quality of life notwithstanding.
Standing, beside you in avoidance of emptiness:

'Whereof one cannot speak,'
that is to say
translate.

11

The intimate acts of the body
are a private thing
    not wholly caught
on film or the stills of pornography

and yet
'a sweet disorder in the dress'

and in the viewer's eyes
and in the public nature of the act

the snap of garter or a run
is irony.   The body's beauty

lives beyond the nature
of its intimate acts.

Home movies document
our social contract and our family loss.

These pornographic stills are hard to date
because they are a mirror and an art.

They document the public nature of our intimate acts
they show the humor in the sweetness of a crotch.

12

I love you
for sentimental reasons, he said,
and those same reasons
are why I live alone.
    I mean:
nothing is in the present tense
and that be not accurate which is immediacy.

This
is my first affair, she said
so please be kind.

To each his own:

you've the soul that snaps my control
(or) I'm a creative play-thing.

13

And if I saw the Harbor Lights my friend
or your face as a glowing substitute
until the lights were lost in the fog
and became one light
    or possibly
only your face now

standing, as you are on the pier
   assuming
   I am in a boat coming at you
your face, therefore, a beacon.
And if you stood still
tall as you are, your face at light level
what sense would it make or difference
that it be a face in the light, or a light
or a face of light, but
   that it guide me.
It matters only
to be able to say it.

14

These days it is not difficult to feel.
Look at the Images
processed into a fine edge
of sentiment.

   even the cars you buy
   are touched by women
the simplest cereals
eaten for sexual gain.

And we are allowed joy in groups
laced with self-knowledge, directed
back into childhood

   sanctions allow us
   even the touch of our own sex.

No, not left or loosed
into the possibilities of weeping,

but that it is a recorded gesture
we can talk about.

We are never alone anymore,
nor need we fear
being caught up
in the accident of sorrow.

15

Speech, being what it is
a term of distance
    nouns of The Intimate Letter
made for a face standing
only in memory
                I speak
anyway, and that's a trust
a perfect burden.

What does it matter
if you listen,
that I sign "Sincerely"?

Dear Sir or Madam,

that letter you forgot to send me
that you hand it to me
    blushing, hoping
I'll read it elsewhere.

16 *(for P. B.)*

Death is a Bitch's Brew, goes
around or under us
cuts our legs out as we go
unheeding
        to the Bijou
or down the street for a friendly
harmless drink.

What can any of us
imagine: stop smoking, drinking,
get in a box?   Locks also protect against
nothing.
        We can avoid
traffic, the small marvels of travel,
sex (possibly) fame (certainly)
money and love, but

not if they bear up the song.
THAT is not possible.

17 *(after Sassoon)*

After a while the dead come back to haunt us
(in a manner of speaking) we say
I'm sorry that it had to end this way.

We mean their lives of course
and that's a burden.
They're dead and gone beyond all care and feeling.

Once upon a time there was a war
and that was painful.

Even as I say these things the Moon gets Blue.
I'm getting sentimental over you.

18

If you will bring me that peach—
If you will just bring me
            that basket of fruit,
cross the room, those flowers—
Then I will kneel.

If you will bring me
your severe body, ribbons, your leather
garments, the straight plumb of your walk
Your strange energy—   Then
I will behave myself
Kneeling.

Stand here for me.

Call me your father. Say:
'my father'
    call me 'a bad boy', only
touch me, brush

into me.

Bleed for me. Drain
yourself for me.

(If we could just watch ourselves, just
being ourselves
in this strange movie.)

19 *(from Krafft-Ebing)*

Gorgeous the night Gorgeous the false stars
on the ceiling, painted, your black room
smell of leather and rancid oil
    and our makeup Gorgeous and black.
I'm a stag, your green contact lenses
Gorgeous of incense & candle, the real
black night thru venetians a dark green.
Handle of no whip
  but of velvet, your glove pulled, half-
moon cuticles of white on your scarlet nails.

I stood among a host of friends and was wounded.
You went out to meet people and they turned away.
Strangely do we touch Gorgeous who were once shunned.

And we speak our rules, "Animal Woman"
you call me "White Stag" bring a basket
plum, apple and pink rose, jar of honey.
    Do we circle Do you call me the magic name
here, the black room turned to white light cooking
Gorgeous against all pain of surprise.

20

Dickies under the jackets of schoolboys
Cheeks pressed in the eaves of houses
a nail head, a chair's legs
I stood at the foot of the mountain.

That's where your father hit me with his hatchet
she said. *Oh, right in the cunt,* he said.

I complimented her on her dickie
and she blushed.

You held the head of my spike in your fingers
You stabbed out with your velvet stiletto
Squeeze my cherries you said
my cherries.

She blushed when I complimented her on her dickie
her knees gathered the body of the cello
You sharpen your soft arrow
on the soft blade of my hatchet

I stand at the foot of the bed.

21

A little loving is a dangerous thing,
a weak knowledge; taste is
finally uninvolved.

A child has an aversion to spinach
he has not eaten. A man
leaves the theater after the first act.

A little loving is a sure thing
to determine freedom
uninvolved.

Taste stands firm against bondage:
a dangerous thing.

All true knowledge is carnal.

22

Put the anchor in the prow of the boat
the boat planes quicker
given the weight.

   Up front
are intricate ways
an increase of speed
understandable notions.

Think
of *the weight of a man's life*
kept in a balance.
Never stand up in an open boat.

Like a term torn from an argument
the boat planes quicker, crosses
the lake at a distance
full of intention—

      (this flat body of water)
      (a singular island.)

A man I think it's a man stands up
in an open boat in the middle on balance
full of intention—a term torn
from an argument
or

his long hair
caught, in the grinding engine.

23

I came to wonder, where had I got this song?
Spikes of memory press
        of a weight of hip on leather
only one phrase at first
(a shadow figure)
minus the lyric.

And we were standing
under a clear sky in the country
watching the moon thru binoculars.

It is never isolate of song full blown
into consciousness, the ultimate
false sense of judgment
of the quality of such things.

        It was Brubeck,

it was *I'm in a dancing mood,* a brief
variant of phrase on an alto sax,
juice of her wise body
I was in.

Dumb and exultant
we watched the moon come round in binoculars
we were touching against each other
this snatch of a song came to me.

It is never isolate, never
a man sitting in aesthetic distance
listening to good music: Byrd
the early Armstrong;

it is continuity.
Brubeck,

specific tilt and figure of a room
in a history, or talk

of the full moon
which is certainly
not art.

24

Given the concerns of these times
so common
                of the way men compromise
themselves and their friends,
strange
that all is not vanity.

Their wives
are excluded from the act,

so sad
that we cannot imagine
        that they touch each other, even
that they tilt toward each other
in public places.

    And we lead our lives,

O Jaded
that we see each one
like a structure of belief
    like an agency,

so common
at this point in time.

25

If I see blood I will take blood,
if a sad case made for lovers
an extraction, a black hole,
I am easily incited.

Friends die and relatives die
and one goes into the street on occasion
and accepts any philosophy.

Deny it: cracked sidewalks,
spit, the real and insane
lovers of garbage, crude signs

and flowers, and beautiful women,
truly beautiful women.

Incited: 'she
who doth walk lightly in the midst of garbage'
(no good song is an argument.)

The blood came from her mouth
it was beautiful: that arc
ah! that color.

26

...in which my hand took yours and placed it
on my body, a risking
no less difficult than the touch
tho I divide them

structured
into a manner of speaking
that is not touch, but distance

your hand, that withdraws itself
more or less into language

richer than gesture.

27

It is not that lives are as plastic,
the new rich provided
by sweat of hard work with money.
It is not usury.

The pen aches and the paper
aches, and the rich go forward in cashmere.
It is not lust or technology.

Good things
and the lack of them,
women and men snowed under:
the days of our lives,

a clear weight of substance
within which floats a snow field
but of roses!

Today I admired the crystal
the plastic holder

and had no power to avoid.

28 *(a coda)*

Tired of words, the indirection of the times,
that enter into the body and make it sick.
Informed, that people quit their friends
for politics instead
    of sex or a new life, fundamental
in its change—no way moving
out do we come to song, but rhetoric.

That place I met you first is still alive
in memory at least
one place of solid structure we can trust
although it lead us
    forward into complexity and lack.

Together we carry a double burden
of dismay, our backs
    are hunched
and bending under it.
It is a load of words, not song, but shit
no marrow oozing from the bones that bear it
    up—my love: time and imagination is our lives'
deceit, discretion when we should be bold
leads into waste and caricature.   But

that I take your sweet smell and your ointment
into my mouth and ears, and wash away
my eyes' tricks and the foolishness
called subtle wit & judgment, fill
my self with body's cure
and with its silence and with skin
until I can sing again.

THE FLORENCE POEMS

The Florence Poems

For Morris

1–Grave Side

I come here not
to bring you back
    tho it be heart-felt
& pathetic,
the insane wish:

two sisters
sitting on a blanket, alone
on the beach in the sun—
gone.

It is also selfish, all
so that a world's particulars
in which I was standing
every day every day
remain (mine),

& against that killing
talk of community
as if we were not always
alone.

The uphill light
biting at the permanent stones
is capricious too.

I am thinking of our secret names.

2–A Domestic Song

He who brings home the bacon is often
lost in the fire that smoked it.

He himself is the fire
& cannot pull his eyes back far enough to see it.

He lifts a glass to her
who is a coat rack for his riches.

She waits the days out
under the smoke clouds of their arrangement.

But the man who is the bacon
doesn't dance or sing her praises.

And whatever god it was that snatched her
is cursed with conviction.

She was no coat rack
this was no arrangement.

All his riches
become dross in proof of her value.

He can only be the other man
in passing.

3–At Ryder

The two women
on the beach

in the sun
    are waiting for someone,
or else resting
after activity: a few shells,
some dusty miller
& two nice stones on the blanket
        which curls a bit at its edges
in just a very light breeze.

But I make assumptions falsely
about postures —younger
than my mother, older than my wife—
    they are not between things,
they wait for nothing,
are not resting,
if
they are in anything
it's 3 children playing in the sand,
the 6 gulls riding
    on the cold swells
beyond them.

The white woman & the black man
stroll calf deep in the surf,
    parents of these variously shaded children;
the man is coal black,
his wife's a little pink at the edges;
staying
between the children & the deeper water,
they splash a little
& play there.

And down the sandy path from the parking lot
a tall young woman in a large red hat
maneuvers a wheelchair

containing a thin old man
in a blue swimming suit
& comes to the water's edge;

she locks the wheels;
he rises a little
       on thin arms & slips
awkwardly into the surf
              where he is turned gently
& starts a slow & graceful sidestroke out
to where the gulls sit.

At the edge of these current events
the two women
       begin to prepare for leaving.
A strong breeze rises up
& all the blankets along the beach
begin to wave.

4–Another Domestic Song

Nothing becomes so difficult
that we can't live with it,

even the way you shift
& turn your carcinoma in the night
with resignation.

The last thing a man wants to do
is the last thing he does—
& other glib words.

Because it was so difficult
he left the room again:

no place to rest his eyes
not even outside
not even closing them.

Because it is so difficult
he entered your room again

—nothing but glib words.

5–The Allergies

The cat sits in the sun
on the desk
                cleaning herself,
her pupils gathered;
in the place
she sits the hair she gracefully
kicks up
            settles around her
    in the sun's
shadows.

In the sun
all energy she has becomes
the innate mechanism:
her long tongue
& her years of sitting
in other places
always in the sun.

I sit again in this room
waiting for voices that don't arrive.
    There is a certain
fragility I've come

to expect in the lives of other people
& now my own;
I've put a thistle feeder
close by
        in the open air,
probably the wrong place:
no birds—
you get what you pay for.

    Listening for other voices:
that twig in the bathroom window
hitting & scraping against the glass—
what else to remind me of
but change
& its attendants: death, & the very edge
of spring's coming
buds, & then green leaves.

If outwardly
the sea right now
    seems misted over,
it's these cat hairs
hanging a kind of woven garment
in the air
between some vision & the bay.

About thirty yards away
some orioles flit
in the skeletal bush
I couldn't see yesterday morning;
    fogged in & raining,
I stayed in most of the day
adjusting the pots under the leaks.

But the orioles strike out together
gaudy in flight
    (their orange armor) quaking
the dead bush as they leave it
in parody of life,
& the cat turns her head in her preening
& we both watch it—
putting it off.

To think of the structure
of the roof only
    when the rain comes in:
I mean
here in the sun,
like the body's barriers,
shingles wear in the grooves
insidiously, in that we do not see it
or do see it
    & put things off—
put what off?

Smoke curls from the cigarette in my hand;
the cat's hairs curl in the smoke & sun:
    you would have been nervous by now,
your fear of cats,
that innate mechanism,
your vision to the bay cut off.

The backs of my hands
are a little like shingles: a field called
lichen planus,
the cause of which isn't known:

I touched
my grandmother's back

in her cancer bed
& then my hands turned red.

I think I am now in a field, called
Anaphylaxis.

Like a planet
(Jupiter, the astronomer says)
burns away in its dark location in the sky,
you had to die
a little distantly & alone,
    & the rest of us
cooked in our allergies
in this foreign place.

    It's brought home every day, that
fundamental thing
we have put off;
now under this high thunder cover
I itch for reclamation of such
waste.

Like in
plants growing on a shocked plane,
    heavy seeds blossoming in the pores,
the innate mechanism of growth,
the backs of my hands
shine sometimes;

imagine
a man standing
with palms over his face;
in that privacy,
in fog,
he'd be a red warning beacon,
putting you off.

No one to talk with anymore
about certain things,
that little
history we had, of which
surely the larger history
is made:

       flavors of ice cream, flowers,
movies & politics,
the singular
cuttings that we made
into the woven textures,
opening the air
a bit at least
to a kind of sighted
human matrix.

I think now
of the flavor of Michael,
   about six summers ago,
turning red in the surf at Longnook—
his intended wife, the seemingly
bright coming of his life—
     now hung from a tree
three days ago, by his own hand
in accordance with some law
of medicine;

not Christ's priests,
philosophers,
nor psychiatrists can put it off,
   nor the spectacle of its effects,
that strange affinity among us:
growth of body & mind
gone wrong,

& the small taste
on the backs of my hands—
Flo,
the little histories
& the large:
such the law.

I see
the boats out on the bay now
    turning in the sun;
the light
even at this distance
glinting off them.

Red sails in the sunset,
but it's morning:
    the sails are white,
the sea's blue-green,
yellowish clouds.

At horizon
a bank of fog, a hazy
demarcation, a soft line at which
the eyes unfocus
& the sea quits.

Are we better out of it?
Is there less pain there?
Why do we
put it off: what is the law?

It's 8:15; the sun
begins
    to give up; the sky darkens
even the dark thunder cover

pressing against it;
it starts to rain.

I place some pans in the house
for the rain that is falling
inside,
& the cat moves from the window
into artificial light;
    even in the rain
your finches have discovered the thistle.

Soon enough
I will have some songs to sing.

Flo,
I begin to think
only these carcinomas
don't put it off.

I've placed my hands into that field
& can join you now.

6–The Tail

The kids across the road
are flying kites this morning
in the fog.

Usually
when the fog comes
it's very still,

but there is breeze enough this time
and they rise quickly and go
almost out of sight.

Standing
mostly in the same places
on the ground

the kids themselves
often disappear
and then return again;

somehow
the invisible kite strings don't tangle,
the kids aren't fighting.

For space,
for a little time
within that space, we continue—

about a mile away
some dogs are fighting
in space and time;

the kites continue
to appear
in the air.

This comes on the tail
of finishing
 a poem for you;

you keep coming back like a song
I'll continue to sing
and keep you alive.

7–Another Song

The places where you lived
& their information:
    you in the medicine cabinet,
in the Scotch broom along the house,
a spot of blood on the bed's undercarriage
insidiously left behind,
& the razors in your clothes.

Poor philosophers,
we long for a ceremony of some kind,
& then rain comes out:
    the gurgle of water in the leaders
whose name is also
Flo.

And the river rises in the rain:
specifically
    the Pamet River
running from Ballston to the Bay
& back again
             (in rain & tide)
a kind of ceremony
I'll make nothing of.

Inadequate philosophers—
It seems so strange:
you are a kind of
    constancy against change.

The rain gives you up
& an iron sun comes out
& with it wind—

you're there in the damp & golden brush
in hints of the little golden birds

in the brash air.

8–Getting Up Again

   I don't really pretend
      to understand it, Florence:
gin in our drinks,
sitting in your back yard among flowers,
            some cheese & crackers on the tray,
& the hundreds of little eyes
of the new blueberries
looking at us;

   we're laughing & talking—
about fishing,
about some of our nutty experiences
in the close past or distant;
we may well go to the movies later,
or stay here
& get a little drunk.

Some shriveled leaves
at the edge of the blueberry patch—
the cultivation marks
of the tent caterpillar—
get me to remember a young child dying
when I too was a child:

the story of blue paint under his nails
his mother had wept at seeing
as he lay in the coffin—

some tangle of difficulties there
a few days before
when he was alive & mischievous—

How cut the pain from such ties,
give back life to the living?
…whenever she hears of crib-death,
& all the chipped paint in the world
reminds her.

But all the little dusted eyes of the blueberries—
almost at the edge of my tennis shoe,
        ready to be picked & eaten—
pull at my gin-pushed gluttonous appetite
& I can't stay with that past
& be appropriately sad right now.

It is also true
that the boy's mother is now around sixty,
has seen her other children grow up
& be happy.
She lives in Hawaii.
        Who can deny she weeps about him at times,
but who can begrudge her
the warm pleasures of that island?

This place seems like an island too sometimes
        (so close to the sea & bay);
it's hard to pass up the colors of the changing surf
as the sun hits it,
& there are days when gulls
& the windy sand veils on the dunes
can take your mind away.

OK:
this talk of islands
turns me to thinking about the girls
taking their swimsuits off at the nude beach;
I've just enough lustfulness in me today
to attend to them,
    but the gin helps
flip my attention to the beach itself
& backward to other beaches,
in California, & a soft high school
oasis in Arizona.

I'd gone swimming with the one I loved that time;
it was very hot; the raft sat
in the middle of the lake,
    & we stroked out to it;
it was far enough,
& we were alone out there
under a dry sun.

I was just 14;
I loved her a lot,
    but had never touched her;
she lay with her soft arm against mine,
& that was almost enough for me.

After we'd cooked for a while,
I got on my elbow & looked down at her,
was moved by the onyx
& copper choker she wore:
    it was half dry in the sun;
it looked cool & hard
on her pink baby skin—

only in color
was it like the necklace of yours
that Miriam has.

OK, Hello,
here I am thinking of you again.

I drink my gin
in the presence of the flowers
you planted & tended,
then turn to the way Morris will tend
your grave
only about a mile away.

    I'm sad & teary for a moment or two;
then turn to the way
we talked about that mystery novel
with such pleasure;
then I begin
thinking of Miriam, & *her* jewelry
on *her* skin.

I suspect
some approximation of this
happens in the heads of all of us;
    I can see the way these blueberries turn
& ripen in the sun;
some of them are still blood raw—
immature, invulnerable
& tasteless—

it's the softer ones,
that are dusted robin's-egg blue,
I lust for—

I'll keep trying to say goodbye to you
so I can say hello again.

9–Whales

In the morning
when the air seemed ancient
in the room where lovers' lamps had burned,
he woke
to discover her absence in the bed:
at first light it was
his dramatic hand entering
that empty space.

And also
as in a cheap movie or novel
the rumpled sheets & stale air,
the moral in the transience
of the bright fire
of their short wicks;
    the perverted message
mildly attenuated in the particulars—
lamp, table & bed—
change coming in small doses
until it seems like constancy.

And so he might have been lonely,
might have risen & gone to the window
thinking he saw light there
or the evidence of it:
    illumined smoke fog of the morning,
not lamp's light
but the first hint of the sun.

The whale lay on the beach in low water.
It was the size of two houses
seen against the men's activities:
some carrying torches,
     yellowish fog lights in the mist,
illumined the ones cutting the melons out
& the vague sense of initials
carved in her head.
        They were all busy,
but it was the whale's
fruit & her presence
commanding them.

And he stood at the window
full of rage & loss—the emptiness
of his private bed behind him,
     the work of the poachers on his beach—
& searched the initials for the name of his adversary,
but it was too foggy:
the carving was only an emblem,
strange & figurative
cut in her head.

I see all this thru eyes
of the sad lover in the window,
     him who I have half-created;
tho he be hazy & unresolved,
he's therefore real,
like the people I live with daily
& know as well.

The literal source
is an old photograph of the beach
above Fisher
     (circa 1890)

in which at low tide the sand
is covered
with beached Pilot whales,
& a dozen or so men,
too well dressed for this place,
are walking among them
& seem startled,
as if shopping
in some new store.

Where does the head end,
& where does the body begin?

    They placed the benign mandibles of whales
upended, as arches of entrance
into the yards of boat captains—
marks of vocation,
& maybe reminders of fear & conquest—
who walked close to the jaws
of whales
many days, for business

(…as if whales grew under the ground
& died coming out
    fighting to leave it).

In Magritte's magic
animated movie
a fabulous whale steers to the shore
    where a man in a bowler (the poet of course)
waits.
The whale beaches herself;
she opens her mouth:
a flower grows on her tongue;
Magritte picks it,

& the whale
winks.

And I think it was night-hunter Spider
who came upon a sleeping whale on the Ivory Coast
& didn't know it—
                    "Well,
          may be some treasure trove in this cave"
& he went in & the whale swallowed him
& it swam away.

And Spider saw the bones of the others digested
& he took the torch that he carried
& held it under the spine of the whale
     where the whale's life source was
& the whale
started to die & rock toward the shore
& it rocked Spider to sleep.

There's a movement against change in the Sea
& Spider slept for a long time & distance
& woke finally to the sound of activity:
     men outside
who were cutting the whale up for gain
& the knives coming in close to Spider
like in a magician's box.

And so he lit his torch
& held it under the whale's spine again
& the whale gave up
     a last yawn at the tickle—
& Spider burst out of the whale's wide mouth
like a warrior
& the men were startled
& thought him the dead whale's

avenging spirit & they all ran away;
  & Spider owned the fruit of the whale
that had eaten him.

A wind off the bay this morning
coming in lightly;
  low mare's tails in the sky
with tips up
promising good weather,
something of the shape of whale's spouts
though they lay horizontal—
from giant whales then
struggling
from the ground.

There
are a few boats out there;
it's calm enough for them:
fishing boats & a few with sails
move slowly
  against the horizon
in moderate breeze enough
to push them—
lightly
& yet seriously.

In the old days
before the vacuums of factory boats
  it was stars & fish that steered them:
navigations of head & body, the two poles
pulling them
even to the Georges Bank
for profit—
who came home
literally frozen sometimes

    & stood in snug-harbor,
a room cut in the fireplace
to thaw them.

John speaks
of the gone days of the Traps,
    those indiscriminate devices
that caught everything:
mostly mackerel for gain,
but fish to be wondered at,
    porpoise & dolphin,
even occasional
small whales.
John keeps listing the names of the dead:
the fishermen
along with the fish.

There remain six spheres of influence:
stars & moon
when visible to steer them;
then satellites;
    then hawks & gulls
of profounder interest;
the society of boats sitting on the sea,
and below these bodies
    the source of their living:
the silent culture
of fish.

It is taking me a long time
    to get to the point, Florence,
but the point is complex: has something to do
with the anatomy of a whale,
the issue—

where does the head end,
where does the body begin?

Below the sacred & scarred berm
the whale
    lies awash in the incoming tide
in the evening;
the scars
are the shards of her own body
where they have cut her up;
        what's sacred is beyond the wealth
& the property;
it's these leavings
that are not left—
    they go into the sea with the tide,
into the bellies of fish:
it's a very old story,
but it is hard to take.

Here in the reflections of our own death
is our triumph:
    55 years lived in the knowledge of it,
one & a half in its presence.
Having known it
& then felt it; having turned
to it
& gone on from that:
    the whale looming in our daily presence
dead on the beach.
In the last year & a half
we were with you:
    that was community—
cold solace for the heads of the living,
but this is where the body begins.

With a turn on the substitute log trick—
one in which the living appears dead—
Ninawa,
the Inland Whale, lay silent
in Fish Lake
    waiting for Toan (the bastard child)
to mistake her body for timber
& walk upon it—

difficult to imagine
a log that size,
but it is more difficult
to think of a whale come into our human
presence in this way—

    thus was the power transmitted
that blessed Toan,
that helped him to riches
& the head of the household at Pekwoi.
Ninawa brought him some understanding also,
& he could bury his mother, Nenem
when her time came
with considerable grace.

But the trick of Spider is different
(a man of various illusions,
    who can actually change himself .
into most anything: be born,
die, & be born again).

    It was a trick of light
& surprise
that sent the men running;
they had knowledge of the whale's death
in its stillness,

but they felt guilt in the salvage
(the head & the body):
                                    thus
       when the Trickster Spider
came forth with his torch blazing,
their thoughts went quickly
to revenge magic;
because they'd felt death was an accusation
they were severely stunned
by a circumstance
in which the dead appeared to live again.

When the man turns back from the window
the light is changing
& the lamp at the bedside,
       now that the room's in half shadow
as sun rises,
is found to be burning
& lighting the bed up
where the gone lover had lain.

The shards of the indentations
of the lover's corpse
are still present,
       & he knows—
were the light lower,
the shadows a little more dramatic—
the log trick could apply:
              the head & the body of his lover
alive in the bed again.

But the last
remnants of fog burn away;
the room gets flooded with light,
& the obscuring

mercurial
shadows of drama are gone.

He gets back into the bed,
reaching to turn the useless light off;
he lies down in the place
where his absent lover had slept.
    He can feel the smooth shell of her face
over his own—
he sleeps like a log.

There's a slow closing of light on the bay;
some of the mare's tails
begin to tip,
    & over them
a few larger clouds come in.

But the sun has some fire left
though low in the sky,
    & though the breeze picks up a bit
some of the sails seem still & have
turned red.

The gulls under the satellites
turn slowly now,
under the hawks sitting on the air
above the sea.

The fishing boats with names of fish
on their hulls, still navigate over
where they think the fish are.

    Florence, do the graves
swell up? I know the grass upon them
grows toward the sea;

so do the heads of the coreopsis
followed by their leaning bodies;
so do we.

And I can see what's left of the whales
out on the beach
as the tide comes in;
        as the tide comes in
the flesh cut from their bodies
is lifted away;
the swells cover up the places where the melons were cut;
they seem to be swimming
as they part the waves.

The initials start to become visible
as they seem to move:
        I can see the shards
of our secret names
cut in their skulls.

I imagine us sleeping
in their massive forms:

        Sperm—

Pilot—

Body & Head

10–Our Secret Names

You had a way of living
in the pleasures of this design
        we all seem to accept daily,

but there is none.
I think you were firm in knowing that.

You went on from it,
& had a way of living with each gesture
    & each event, so that a kind
of what I will call wholesomeness
lit it up.

You "lit it up"—
I like the sound of that—
a little like rockets
    blooming over the wharf in P-Town
this last 4th.

So much for the poverty of metaphor:
those brief & impotent sparks
in a dark sky.
    It is of course down here
under the rockets always
that we live
(lived).

The light that touches
the autumn olives in a breeze
can make their leaves glint in the night:
    it is the full moon, but it's
the undersides of the olive leaves
that have the silver.

That's better.
We all share in the power of the light;
at least we own
    a particularity of reflection,

if your secret name
is Luna.

But all this keeps us very lonely
& the moon,
consistent with this language, gets
eaten away,
      & it is only
the aura of its presence
that sustains us
till it comes again to thrill us
back to our privateness.

Flo,
I have tried hard to love you
as I love myself.

Now
into the perfect
community of our isolate lives
I commend you & your secret name,
dear Florence,
& I commend my own.

Still / Quiet

Spring Change

The birds drop tricky out of the limbs,
sometimes a full story
& come to rest
   in lower branches
where the trees grow
against the building.

They are sparrows again, because
sparrows always come again
in any weather.

The trees blow
& change their colorings in the wind
that also changes.
Any season

  is different from the rest,
  but it is no matter.

What we have is sparrows again
sitting & falling
from bare limbs.

They come to rest
while all the rest

doesn't.

A Casual Spring Song

The tree begins to leaf, and thereby
gains a purchase on the wind
    on the terrace across from me.
It leans
the way our avocado does, when sun
circles the building.

    But that is inside,
& the tree
is free in the wind
it shakes in.

My cat sits watching it
    & a woman comes out, in a flowered shift
that blows too, to look at it,

    who glances at both of us,
and we three
turn together
and watch the tree.

Poem for My 38th Birthday

In the last hours of the early morning
of my birthday
    the red dog across the road is howling,
announcing something
I rise too.

Her snout is pitched upward
in the grey sky, her haunches
close to the ground.
    I think she has a rash there.
I go over
and console her.

Coming back across the road
stumbling a little in half sleep
into my 39th year
in enough light now
    to see almost clearly,
the cat mews plaintively in the open window, wanting
an early feeding,
a little atypical
but she gets it.

And then another voice is singing,
quietly at first
at 5 a.m.: "Happy

Birthday to you
Happy Birthday."

(My wife in a half sleep murmuring.)

The birds chatter.
I go out and feed them
and sit and watch them.

Everything is consoled and ordered
and gone back to sleep.

It lightens up—
Happy Birthday!

Looking

No ideas or smart thoughts today
but who knows, maybe
    one sees best
        when the vessel itself is empty.

Out my window, the fat bee hangs
    on the bending rib
of weed and then
walks out to its end
    upside-down
                (the weed
    bent like a bow) then turns himself
    near to the ground,
walks back again
as the weed straightens.
                   He
elevates himself in air
by walking
    and only then does he fly away.

Pigeons
rise too
    like a column of air, and only
when they reach a certain height do they straighten out
and head home.
              And we
are trained in such
metaphor & distinction,

Imagine
       men walking on moving beams
in a city sky,
        and over that

men mixing themselves with sunbeams
     and celestial repairs.

Our cat, now
looks like a lion in the longest grass,
squats, wiggles a little,
chases her shadow,
     then looks at us,

and I confess
     I've done a dance for her
playing the larger cat
in our living room.

And what to make of all this? Why
nothing. Only
meager song to meet them
where they are, and me too, we
two
     linger awhile
as if could share that element
     and we can—

bees
duck in the flower's cup,
some spotted bird
tickles his feathers up,
the grass blows to and fro,

     no ideas but sense of song,

each living thing displays itself
for others and its kind—

     we do too.

Brother Moon

I ignore you Brother Moon so long
before I know
you're back again

It's night)
and in the living room she stood
enchanted—
                    or at least
she got up for you
at 3 AM.

         At 9 she tells me
how you shone for her.
I was asleep,

and now her gown's opaque.

Just This

Here
in quiet of early morning
looking in
to a city back yard of no expanse
some light enters—
    its consequence
in the finely tuck-pointed mortar
of red brick, above
her window—
& then she begins to turn.

4 twisted gingkos
in this small & suddenly
lit space,
    their branches active
& their twigs some-
times touching one another
the way we do sometimes, & 4 birds
sparrows) too.

Maybe
we could put it all together, may
be the light joins us, but is
only a reflective quality.

Of the things discovered
it is she, her turns
    to get coffee ready;
not brick or light
trees or the quiet birds
begin it.

I make
some coffee too
for you
before day starts in earnest
to confuse it.

Birdsongs

Sparrow

The lone sparrow comes
and settles in on the feeder
as the light fails
us and her.
    She is pregnant,
allows us
to come close enough to see that, and when
we are almost
      too close
she moves off: twig, to another
twig to a branch
cross space, to another tree.

Her movements are economical;
she watches

us, and we too watch
as if her life mattered
  we stand there
in regard of her namesake, the small
sparrows in her;

it is no coincidence
we lack mastery.

We call it grace or the absence
of grace,
    insouciance,
fact of the mother
swollen to her instinct to rest:
the nesting urge.
She watches.

And in the morning he rises
        complicatedly beside you
from clarity of sleep, puts
bare feet on cold floor;

who is the simpleton?

The hawk will eat her
in regard of his namesake;
her bones crack
brittle, spectacular in her death

to us
who watch her
        flammable in shadow
(which obscures her)

we are the fire.

Yellow Bird

Early morning. It is so quiet.
Yellow bird
lands on the feeder's rest
five feet from me.

I can hear her claws, can see
her way of movement along the rough doweling,
see the whites of her eyes.

She sees me,
hears my rough smoker's cough,
or feels some energy in
my sense of surprise
at her closeness, & then she flies off.

At once,
in the quiet of the early morning
I feel my losses in the loss of her.

    Is that her
    sharp and melodic voice
    in the distance? her presence,
    wholesome, because it is out of reach?

She had
a white head. Her claws
were yellow too.

She couldn't stay here.

Night-Light

The birds kick
and sing their energies in the night;
    they become a nuisance:
are they
night birds, are they somehow troubled,
what do they have to complain about
their lives?

I can't sleep, feel
maybe I'll never sleep again;
was it too much coffee, is there
something on my mind?

They squawk and sing,
they are very close
    to where I try to rest,
they are local.

I could not find them even
in this full moon.

Maybe
it is this light
that keeps us up.

A Very Hot Day

The sparrows catch the light, and look
yellow in the sun.
    One sits on a branch and turns
his breast into it.
He shines
like layered bronze as the sun hits him
and swells up a little to meet it.

You come out of the shower shining
and powdered, to defeat it.
You are not bronze
    but pounded rings of powder plate your body.
You turn your powdered breasts
back from the window.
You sing enough to keep this tribe together.

Rocks

That I had not known enough then to cure it.
Had there been more time, my father
a matter of learning
　　　loss of innocence—
but the fat pills
like footballs, choking you.

A friend and geologist had
not known much of poetry
but had known rocks:
　　　"They're alive!" he said,
but he wrote poems like a virgin.

This morning
birds come I have never seen before: blue
and fat, and I grab the *Field Guide*
too late.

To lead one's life is to lead
but to follow,
as if that book in the head
flipped through
　　　but the birds left in the meantime.

My friend, the geologist, has since learned to write.
The rocks were alive tho
and have since changed appearance.

Turns

I want to be happy, for you
to be happy
too,
    is not always a possibility.
Daily
something discovered
that was not there yesterday,
but the mood's the same—

a single boat
moves on the bay
within my scope too far for color.
    It's blocked out suddenly
    behind a bush 10 feet away—

    trees, bushes, bees,
this year
indistinguishable insects
buzz in the new-cut grass.

To be happy: defined
certainly by a state of mind
    unaffected sometimes
by what is seen:
that
is certainly
    sickness, we all have—

and should we
want the world the same?

It shall not be,
is at once too glorious and too

cruel
        in its insistence: demands
us *to be happy*, gives
back the dead each year come alive
birds too various for names
17-year locusts

in our heads. And here
the bush moves and the boat's
back again, still single
turning its red sides in the breeze

while
the day turns
        and the wind turns
                my head

while flowers turn, with the sun
their cells on that side dying
their open faces
turn, against our foolish needs.

Faces

Inch by inch
the rain comes in off the bay
  rolls in in a changing cloud
folds of the clouds face,
ripples of brow
                crosses
    the acres of space between
  my face in a window
the bay's submerged profile.

Someone
is maybe walking the bay's beach now
unseen, where it may
    be clear, watching
the newly revealed clarity of blue
sky above it. There
may be birds there.

2 faces, one able
only to see thru a 3rd face in the glass now
beyond where, what
    elegant figure walks on the beach?

    it is myself
    it is an old friend
    it is some past
      lover in her perfection, is
    noone I know or remember
    has nothing to do with me
      is maybe not there at all. That may
    be its elegance.
    Dissolved & broken

the cloud forms into fog
                              into wet air.
Finally
the bays beach reveals itself
subtly, changed in its shift of sand.

There is no one there.

The fog closes again.
My face in the window,
rain on the pane.

Some Small Movements

The sparrows lift
and flock together in the rain.
Before the rain, after a very stormy night
the sodden tree they sat in
   threw its drops around, but they
were not windswept until it rained again
and they went
somewhere.

Even in the rain
the sparrows seem very dry;
they don't shine, but they do
preen a bit when they have time
when they come back again to the tree.

The sparrows don't have much time; their small
frenetic bodies cook and discover
and quit even the most intricate task
quickly, and they flock together often
and go someplace
it seems only the better to return again
to this tree.

Now it is raining.

The sparrows grow limpid
   and huddle together; the tree
grows weighty from its burden of sparrows and rain
and a few drops slant into my window.
It's as if
there may be something to talk about here.
Then a little sun breaks
and the sparrows flock again.

Gulls

The gulls come farther inland when it rains
as if the sea itself
   in its deposits on the land
were there. They drop
and swoop to fish in the longer grass
         then bank
   and rise up puzzled before they hit
then move away
till they get high enough to see
the final demarcation of the land,
then drift
   then hold themselves
in that location.

   /

My heart s in the highlands too sometimes
my body also turned
         to whatever job or pleasure,
   the mind gets lost
dips, and returns again
to you: my Sea of Tranquil Waters.

   /

Always
driving past the dump
we see gulls lining the largest hills,
a string of pearls like wisdom
   halfway between
the garbage and the sea.

Moot

It is not true that things remain,
though, in the ultimate
it is true
          (a useless knowing, but
that it bear us up).

The fact is
different grasses fill each pace,
exchange.
          The birds this year
are not the same as last,

had we but sense
of their generation, could we but mark
their separate faces
as our own
returns here, yet grows older.

The fact is that the grasses seem
to blow the same,
each bird
turns round familiarly,

   lest that we look too close.

It is some way our selves remain.
What we left is gone.

WE ARE THE FIRE

The Trumpet Vine

This plant that rises
    pushing itself snake like
against the house
is honeysuckle,

  & it reaches up
to find some purchase
    on the shingles & tucks
its small & delicate
toy trumpet flowers in there—

it smells good
but is just as easily identified
by sight.

On the other hand
I never saw the trumpet vine
    (easier by far to recognize
when it's in bloom)
that grew along your porch
& covered a good portion of its roof
when I was young.

I never lived in your house
but I spent a good deal of time
coming & going.

Away from there to here
where I can see
    beyond their constant names
even the change in
delicacies of weeds in my yard

& the new bucklings
in the trees from winter winds,

I have to wonder
how I spent those years
    passing the unseen trumpet vine,
my head usually down
& elsewhere.

Always
it seems better in the past;
it's very hard to live
where body is
    & I get startled when I think
I didn't know you well at all
& that some details of this yard
      will inevitably escape me
leaving only
partial understandings.

On the other hand
    the trumpet vine
tho once cut back by accident
is curling still
      while we're away
sending its clear flowers out;

they may well bloom for someone else
who may also
be missing them.

I mean to say
I could have danced
with horns behind my ears;

we could have danced together
snaking the vines on our arms.

At least I wore your bathrobe once
& made you laugh;
    the doctor told you no intercourse for two weeks
when you were 82,
& we both laughed.

At least
I have your blood in my vines—
I mean my veins…

Theme Music

When they play theme music from *The Godfather*
I am genuinely moved.

The movies are amazing.

The way at the wedding at the Galaxy
we drift together
in tux and white dress on the dance floor—

well, I am born free &
Is this the little girl I married?

On the screen, in the movies, the people
drift in and out of relationships
of places: Miami-
           Sicily-Havana.
Some are pulled backward through open drapes
onto balconies, to the sound of music, they
double up and bow.

At the Galaxy, they play
theme music from *The Way We Were*
      memories/light the corners of my mind,
dancing
with you in my tux I am born free
into the movies.

But *The Way We Were*
is not the way we were
ever,
      and in the movies
people die and return again,
a pair screw standing up against closed doors

at the wedding,
    a man wakes up sleeping
with a horse's head.
And here, at the Galaxy
a hush falls
    over the darkened room.

To the beginning strains of theme music
from *The Godfather*

the bride and groom,
whose moves are anticipations of tragedy
    (but in a movie)

dance awkwardly
into their song.

Standard–4, These Foolish Things (Residual)

Each time I see a crowd of people
    (evidence of a lost chance of mastery)
standing at a stoplight at Flatbush Avenue—
possibly
it is raining—
reminds me of you.

    & the ghost of you sings.

We
winged it in the nature of Country & Western
dark bars in Corpus, you
    sweet bucktoothed Mexican girl
      hugged in the arc of parking lights
      lit up the beach and the Gulf of Mexico
foolishly.

An airline ticket to romantic places?
Chicago,
braces of high-school sweetheart
  cutting the lips
    not the time or place
inappropriate.

What goes on daily
the impropriety of staring
    flint of heartland straight into
the dead center of the heart, is
flesh memory,
cleaved in twain.

Each time I see a crowd of people
the light changes

the ghost of you sings
inappropriate,
              out the classroom window
maybe you'll be there:
hair tied back in a ponytail
walking the bright side of the avenue

going away
from this talk of a Black African
growing-up story:

      "He held
      Njoroge's private parts
      with a pair of pincers…"

you / in a variety of gowns and faces

—these fragments
—these foolish things.

I want something.

Standard–5, I Can't Get Started (The Fan)

I need a little coffee
but I'll take a little satisfaction instead.
Bright morning, a clear head
seems appropriate
    but I'm a little messed up rising
    from a troubled sleep, cough up
a few mechanical tears in the cutting wind
going out to write this.
I could use a little flushing of the system
to get started.

  last night
  we walked the streets of P-Town much longer
  than I'd thought possible
  given my oyster legs & sore arms.
  She paced me
  carefully, into the shops
  and I stuck with her
      hardly able to even have eyes
  for the passing women.
  I was so tired, we thought
  we'd go see *Female Trouble* at 10
  but she could see my slump,
      we decided against it & came home
  & read a little & got to bed late.
  I must have dreamed
  but I don't remember.
      My head's a little clearer now.

The Eastern-
King-Bird sits on the bayberry stalk before me;
he's clear of eye. The pleasure
      of his body is like a bird-book

picture, the demarcation
of wing color and beaked head. He fled
from the feeder which was too close to me.
He sits looking at me
        from a little under a safe distance
were I a cat. Does he know this?
Of course he does:
probably the size distinction. Turns his head,
feathers slide and meld on his neck
like a rich feathered fan.
        How do you think the forms
of fans were invented, anyway?
The Royal Fan—The King Bird.

Seaward—where
there is nothing but fog cover
a few miles out
under
a day moon, Factory Boats
& the local fishermen dropping their nets
        that fan out catching
whatever is left,
where it is clear (no
Sea of Remembrance)
while the cat hunts here
& the birds too.

Would
that we could
old friend, have lived
something akin
to these
        half casual motions
quiet, lighter
than we were

(hunters also)
turned in
to relationships:

wing fan passing over the bird's sharp eye
for a moment; the cat makes her move,
bird lifts
and settles in again as she passes,
occasional eye shade of the fan.
      I need a little satisfaction
        but I can't get started.

I remember the picture of a woman sitting
on a sheet-draped couch,
      your wife naked and posing, holding
a fan maybe (stripes
of Venetian light) and then
that Western bar painting you made from that:
white sheets turned to satin
or blue silk against
her whiteness, her new fullness, hair
a little longer
      than her hair
(in starlight) that
modest guarding
of fan discarded, turning
discomfort in the snapshot
to ease.

      What was it you wanted to give me?

a little intimacy? a twist
of relationship?
some satisfaction?
or female trouble?

charted—

Fans flash under the sea catching
the light
        off fish;
there are two birds now, the third
a cat; that
revolution of species
did not succeed
tho, she is flushed out.

As if oiled,
the body in the painting
on velvet, in surety; I remember
more, old friend
        your delicate art,
the challenge of a little
photographic realism
& romantic handling,
her real passing
along the couch I awoke on
sweating in starlight.

What we needed was satisfaction,
a little eucalyptus in bath oil:
to be object of another's care regardless
of neurotic motive,
love, or the fact
that her head was elsewhere, she'd
bring us tea,
the blanket and the soft chair,
as if our sickness were physical, and
such care healed.

Now it is raining, there's
nothing in it for rejuvenation,
        it'll soon clear.
The King Birds puff in the wind and rain,
but the sea's clouded.
There's female trouble stirring
in the closest bush.
Gestalt of wing fan breaks
in the passing storm.
        The coffee is cold, half drunk
and unsatisfied.
Fans fold their memories
and the patterns burn.

Started.

We thought to know her better
than we knew ourselves, we did not
        know ourselves, each other
the ones we lived with
(live with)—

        I see her often
not in the painting, in photo
but moon of her ass
        in starlight; in a way
we lived together
in weather: the each
and quiet possibilities of change
within continuity.

Down at the bay
the quay is full of fishermen
and their catch: blues & striped bass,
the passing women in white shorts bending over

the rows of fish,
                    the lovely
silken slime of death on their silver bodies
and on the backs of the women's thighs
oil, mixed with sweat.

A Moral Proposition

She took me to her house and explained
her husband
   was in some way defective
& would I not consider?

I was 19 and ready
to leave next morning for California
(which she knew) she was a nurse,
outside
   it was early evening, no trees
   yet in the project,
ground broken in places for new houses
for flower beds.

I thought Jesus! this is *not* for me, but she
cajoled me—English
they had just arrived here
childless—very starched
and nunlike
in her nurse's dress
& efficient.

Early evening, lights were low, we sat
on the couch together
proper, talked in a soft voice
analytic, and like a mother.

And I was very close
to being convinced, could see
the bedroom thru the door, why not
leave a child here?
Jesus! this is for me, I thought

potency, I thought
this is the perfect gift,
transcendent; she was a nurse
    I was her patient
—she turned to me
a little flushed,

and when I saw her lust
I left.

On the Road to Perry's Farm

Almost naked riding on a bicycle she comes
along the road from Perry's farm.
The basket
over which her breasts bob, carries
some fresh corn
from Perry's. Her bikini
tight on her brown body, willfully
she shifts
    the 10 speed to go
up the hill.
Will
she stall, fall
    and scrape her body, will the corn
spill its yellow grain and silk across the road?

Almost naked
she makes it up the hill.
I enter Perry's farm and smell
dogs & fish.

Standard–7, An Austere Song for Sal Mineo

So easy is the myth of Public Figures
that certain transparency
in which we are amazed to find them.

No sooner does the mind
turn to expansive showplace of vision
in which the child-star is encumbered
but that he grows.

Perry Mason
the fatherly trial-lawyer is effeminate
    raises orchids & gestures
his limp hand
tracing subtle figures in the air

& what truly is age
or masculinity, but a fixity
a way of placement.

Somehow
the breeze today is structured
austere & arch: it moves against the windows
like architecture.
This is a good day for mythology.

In the movies
a distant sound of thunder, a freight train
a music:
    each action is embedded
with music,
guide-light of the myth.

But today is also
a place of private actions of people,
streets of dreams & houses
over which
birds sing their music
& disjunction
in the quality of this air
which does not enter our lives
necessarily, tho we wish it.

Sallie—
I am thinking of a song, some theme music
& a context in which a Public Figure
in my own life is moving
  a young psychotic & rebel
& the song is wordless, the melody
hardly perceptible, but that doesn't matter.

That most poems, too, stand in their way
as fiction, doesn't matter
either.

The face of the past president fails.
It is a sad reminder,
his mother
his good father, & the way
each one falls out of placement
confuses our histories—
that matters.

But I am thinking of the movies, almost
hearing music. You were always
surrounded by songs, rebellious
& moody,
   as if your heart was

more serious
than our hearts, who were
locked in a similar age:

the 50s, those songs
so inextricable from memory, I can almost
hear them
     still as they form
what a heart is,
that false
communality of the past.

But this is no day for weeping & discovery.
It is a day shot thru with sunlight
all morning
     & by afternoon
the people
are half free from covering
half joyful, even tho
they might be going to funerals,
have troubles:

     they live with song.
This is incredible light.

And I am thinking of the movies, almost
hearing that music, you were always
good for a joke:

Gene Krupa, your sweetly ridiculous
age there. Jokes
about casting you as Moses
     in roles of great subtlety
your name used always
derisively, in friendly conversation.

The myth you lived in
was aegis
under which children
of your own age
found what?
    but a placement
& contrast, a charming music:

we were all
adolescent-child-stars
burning in myth—
but that was not you.

Sal,
today's air has a quality like crystal.
You can see right thru it, as if
thru the film's transparency
the music & thunder

  as if it were not mythology
& the newspapers reached & joined you
into character of Brooklyn Street-Youth
now heart stabbed in California.

What a sad
& useless posture we come to
in want of articulate life.

Move over) Let the light air
bird songs, thunder & the music
come down from its invisible structure

to mourn you, Dino:
that was a faker of memory, as if
life were art

regardless of the quality of either,
this was not your life
tho it was ours.

He who lives as a Public Figure is not living
life there. Sal,
I imagine you could have seen with me
into the strange indifference
of today's sky.

It is architectonic & beautiful
like the history of Public Figures

but it is only
a quality of air.

Sitting in Gusevik

I was sitting in my cousin's house, at the start
        of a loss of ten pounds (the fjord
    a block away)
in the middle of the longest day
in Norway.

Some fires would burn on the hills at midnight
(still light) and they'd be setting rafts
of logs ablaze,
tho in avoidance of trout farms,
adrift, across from the steel factory
at Gusevik.

Gusevik, which I
had just found out was my real name
but in this case was a house,

                            outpost
    in which a man and his wife now lived
who had changed his name
when his father'd bought the place
from my cousin, Oskar's father: Ommond Gusevik,
around 1910.
                    I was sitting there.
Outside it was
well (you know) Norway, back
in a time when sex was dirty and air was clean
        where I could see across
my cousin's potato farm
across the road
and a white horse walking slowly
in her fields
close to its time of foal.

We were sitting in my cousin Oskar's house
downstairs, in the coffee shop, his daughter
Johanna, who ran the place, was cooking
carbonnade
        and a drunk came in
who loved her
obviously, had come in
to be close to her, and I
    was still getting used to the fact
my name was no longer Olson
but Gusevik.

The drunk
was trying hard, but he
could get no tumble.

           Johanna
would laugh a little
and scowl and raise her eyebrows
in our direction

         and the drunk
obviously thought
to play to us a bit
and said in perfect English:
"Business is business, but love is bullshit."

Sitting here now in America (NYC)
in this room,
and out this window
snow-capped terrace railings & the slush
already running in the tiles' grate.

Birds
that come this height

are truculent and peck
    at anything that's in sight

blue jays & few
sparrows, stalwart pigeons come to sit
on the refined steel of the water tower.

The cat squats
in danger upon
    the dark ledge, her body
    darker still against
white snow;
crazily
close to death but giving in
to a business sense
she sees the way I watch her
watch the birds;

I see
the old hotel
across from me, the cluttered
minuets
of men and women
    doing business, and the birds
and cat that stand apart from that
and me.

I hit
the ashtray's edge
put down the cup
and think:
    "it's dark here today."

    It's darker still in Norway,
where

in summer we had rowed
across the fjord,
    were almost caught in a sudden Norwegian rain
and sat on the porch of the house in which
my great grandfather was born,

Tobias
upon whose porch I sat
6 years old with a cup of Swedish coffee
in Illinois.

    Memory
like his son and grandson stops
prematurely and like their deaths.

The house is gone, the other
across water,
faces a factory.

Well,
the drunk was saying
    what he thought we'd like to hear,
he had a leer.
His talk was American Ingenuity,
            but he
could not manage well,
and we
were a little uncomfortable. Johanna
finished her cooking up and got rid of him.

We talked
    and left the house at midnight
light of sun still visible
    presence on town street

& drove to the public bonfire
to a vacant lot where it was fading,
   people gathered
around huge ember logs and sang
religious songs.

I hung to the window post, and then
was fading west
to L.A.,

to Lois
who woke me up with tea. It was
the heavy porcelain navy cup
she'd put on the bedstand,
and I
was brought from dream by entrance
into the dream of tea smell.

I was doing business there
with white woman (or) white horse, in haze
of flared nostril smoke,
                    so that
the dream was led by intention
into the presence of Lois,
   (face / in tea haze)
and this
outline
of dream wife
   was sweet horse breath, but then
was tea until
I was awake,
            and Lois
blowing the steaming tea across
my sleeping face

& I was asleep & awake.

Personal history is a dream like that
and like the Indian speaks of what it can't remember
but knows is true, and says
in extenuation of where it started from,
its history: "It is said."

It is said—
the old folks carried
100-pound sacks of grain
in the 19th century
up the steep escarpment behind the house
to the other, older houses above the fjord
        (were very tough
and Oskar said that
when the Nazis came, the food supply got short
and you could see the poor tobacco
the people were forced to grow
flame like tiny torches
in pipes across the fjord.

Today
Norwegian wood
floats in a cove across
from Gusevik beside
        the steel factory in which
Johanna controls the food concessions and the drunk
works, and I
blessed by American Ingenuity
row hard against
the tide from the North Sea
in the face of that,
i.e.:
The Log Cabin
a Restaurant on a Farm
a Name Change.

Lois,
it was a dream as if
the jasmine in the tea were a simple tool,
　　tho magical, that could
unlock some history

as if
the woman in the dream (the horse), her breath
were the real thing, and I
had changed somehow
to a rarity
of feeling where
the tea's technology was a sacredness
in that I was consumed by a history that was
a part of me, was gene-like
and my life,
　　for lack of a better word, was tribal
so that business was
a part of love & cluster
like the valley of Kvinesdal

in which I rowed
　　where everyone was my relative
and write about, as if
there could be answer here

in America (NYC) sitting in Gusevik, my skin
but in this room where lives are only private
& so is love and business.

They were kin,
　were very friendly.
We went to the cemetery,
my cousin's husband took me to a soccer game,
we ate good food.

They certainly seemed to love my wife,
even the doors of their language
opened a bit. The virtue I made of ignorance
of their speech, to nod and smile
and gesture when I could not understand, gave fruit.
Johanna sent me the valley's history book
I could not read.

The scale says I have lost 10 pounds, have changed.
I who had no business within that place.
I of the changed name.

A Frame

Now it is raining.
Its first few drops as always
    slanting against the window
one comes to learn about
just sitting, & then sun comes out
& right away goes in & it starts to rain again
left to right.

I never had a vision. I've had
a few dreams that seemed
possibly significant
    but I wouldn't bet on it.
I think I like that.

Christ! these few
beautiful living objects, leaves
throwing the rain off, 4
relatively huge
    slender trunks of ginkgo,
squirrel touching his damp body against them,
(his dew body).   It's early morning—

not the tales
but the details—
& now the sky darkens & the details
minus obscuring light
are clearer,

distant thunder.
It's going to storm
& the sockets behind me crackle.

My Moon Girl

I took a lady out
into the breath of her own desire,
the obvious melody
of an amusement park, when I was 15 years old.

She had more
craters in her face than I had that year;
she sat near me
in the back seat of the car,
but was hiding her face.

How have we learned to trust, love
be gentle, give out
more than we take back,
treat things other than economic?

She was a blind date, wanted only
a little blindness from me.
        I remember I loved
the ancient
moonscape of her face
she turned toward me
 only in the dark tunnel of love;

I kissed
the umblemished
liver of her soft lips, but I wanted
to touch my moon girl's face.

The Clasp

You were my heart's desire, she said—
　　that same game:
the past tense, divided
self & the public utterance.

　We were at the senior prom and her
necklace kept
falling down into little cleavage
(enuf for me at 18) her mother, always
smiling and fixing the clasp.

But here (16 years later)
it is her mother's face and not hers
draws me to lust.

We always thought you'd be a priest,
the girl says, or a doctor.
I dreamt about you last night.

　Her mother grins over her shoulder,
fixing the clasp.

Cylinders

My neighbor digs in the earth, the rich soil
he has brought together
    there in his garden against the wind.
Under his blue hat, white shirt, and hands
a glimpse of the hearty and large
green leaves, and a little red of the rhubarb
where he is tending
    and bending down to it,
fingers among the stalks.

It's early in June, a late spring,
a few flowers still on the honeysuckle,
first buds
    of portulaca
have not appeared, the weeds
have not gone seriously to seed yet,
    no indoor petals to float—
rose or day lily in bloom—
and we've neglected to buy petunias
for the planter.

We have
the green beginnings of rattlebox,
a little old-field-toad-flax,
a few juniper,
    strut of purple and gold finch,
and two large cement cylinders
(drainage devices) to be set in,
edge of the new road they've cut

    —cylinders for the rain
that won't sink into soil, but sit
glistening and ineffectual

on the new blacktop.
I watch
the hawk float in low over the scrub,
touches of pale yellow, gray and rust,
no more than six feet above it
and close enough. I'd say
    marsh hawk, hunter (harrier),
presage
of what skillful darkness?
It looks like a sunny day at ease, but
cylinders for the rain—
and now a few clouds come in.

   Donna was a little tipsy
   when she came over—
      Papa Joe could die soon.
   He says at the fish store
   "I've got cancer;
          I get the fish for nothing."

The drone of a dozer to my left.
I can only hear it,
but it shakes the house.
It's beyond the frame
I count on.
   Little shakes
to be honest, but ominous
of something—
sure the house'll hold;
it has through many winter winds I hear
in times I have not been here.

      Nor have I seen that river
I got out of you, Becky—
which river? in New York City?

456

But you met boys there,
and one suspects
    from sudden shyness and your smile
to kiss them, hold hands at least,
what? 16 years old?

    You were happy then, but you
seemed always happy: *The Happy Immigrant*,
name for a musical or old movie.
I don't pretend to know
what happiness was about in your terms
exactly ("Mother"?)—
    grief beyond my experience
of grief, but very happy.

A quick wash on the window, the drops
distinct and accountable,
    to bring in, but obscure, light;
there's little of it:
a few clouds draining now,
the tentative
            coming of fog over the bay,
my delicate line of horizon
no longer attenuated, but it's a spring rain.

The cylinders begin to darken on the hill;
the drain holes in them catch light;
the cut of the new road, its primitive
sand, reddens.

    There was a light in Grade's house
    all night; come to find out
    she died yesterday.
    Simply, we had not noticed it
    in daylight.

457

Beyond the cylinders, the houses
on the crest are not for mourning,
    a kind of Polynesian temple at the edge—
would they
import natives if they could,
outriggers
and various structures, to dry fish?

What they have
are two slow draggers in the distance,
    four charter boats
popping for blues, numerous gulls,
wake of a few whitecaps,
and the smoky beginnings of fog.
—(the life of a fisherman?)

    "I've got this cancer;
    I get the fish for nothing."

    "...but he's got breasts like a woman now
    that's not right for a man!"

    (Donna is crying)

There is a new heaviness of cloud cover coming in;
fairy lights on the draggers
blink on;
the charter boats quit and move out;
gulls rise into smoke.
Fog crosses the beach, reaches
    the base of the temple, obscuring it.
Suddenly, it is raining hard.
I see my neighbor
holding his hat brim, ducking
    among the rhubarb,

heading in. The dozer grinds into sight, and has
incredibly, an umbrella.
I think it's going to rain for a while.

For nothing, and yet
for everything in sight, Becky—
you were always happy—
only a few blocks away
from your place and Gimbels
    the clouds break into patterns of light.
Could we have talked about *light footed sparrows*
on the heavy capital at the museum?
I doubt it—

    A few gather here
under needles on pine limb: moments
against wind and rain.
I can see the heads of blackbirds,
spotty, in the drain holes
    in the cylinders on the hill.
The hawk was a large kestrel, no harrier,
but in glide,
a sparrowhawk.

—(Were you always happy?)

Three birds lift
from the cylinder holes,
rise up and circle,
dip, and return again
not redwings,
    they are grackles—
helmets of gun-metal blue
in this little light.

But the delicate drops on that river,
a spring rain,
    colors of what dampened petals?
You, under willows or old oaks,
kisses or hand holding:
we talked about that.

And a new love at 73, and even sex—
but it was not the sex—
was a clear adolescent pleasure,
at 73!

    "He is not talkative,
    not like Jack was;
        he reminds me of Jack though.

    We talk very late at night sometimes;
    we walked out for a soda!"

In the force of the rain, the slow
coming of fog, cloud folds
        that thicken as they move,
the houses look like tombstones on the crest,
but I mistrust it.
    At the crest, they break up horizon,
a few lights in them now;
land cuts, for their rest and prominence;
safe and happy people
inside them:
    Dream Houses, land
reformulated for them. I mistrust it—

I was wrong again—
the clouds
begin to lift and dissipate, the sun burns

the fog away, blue hat
     bobs above the rhubarb again; the dozer
has a crane. It lifts the cylinders;
grackles popping from the holes and rising
indiscriminate, in the sun.

Were you really happy?
I could ask the dozer that. It lowers
     the slowly turning cylinders
into the ground. The grackles
seem unhappy, drift
float and circle, over the fresh holes.

          "...but he's got breasts like a woman now
     that's..."

          a kind of transformation
Donna, he gets the fish for nothing.
He may be happy or sad,
     but that is our indulgence.

It is the deaths that are simple, the lives
and the dying in them
complex: we know nothing in our privacy;
it is enough
that we leave them their own.

Becky
beyond these houses of questionable taste,
now shining under a clear sky,
I give you the sea, which is tasteless,
outside such considerations, only
     it is in words this time.

But I remember
a time, you walked right down into it—
who were afraid of weather—
    in your white patent shoes,
your white nylons, your legs
(yes) like cylinders—

and stood in the very edge of the surf:
the sand sucked your feet under a little,
a wash of white foam at your ankles.

You had your back to us.
On the beach, we were amazed at your boldness,
but that was our amazement.

You may have been smiling, moving,
thinking of the boys at the river.
I don't know.

The fish near your feet were for nothing.
You were a beautiful sight to behold.

Standard–11,
Anything Goes (The Emerald City: A Key)

The first time we got
really close to one another, beloved,
    is when we slept together: your hand
awkwardly on my shoulder
pressing me gently for a welcome
before dropping off
at 24—
now we are 40.

Well,
at least my shoulders remain firm
tho I've sloppy posture,
and last night
walking the streets of P-Town again
a young man tried to accost me.

    Hipless
    in very tight Levis & wide belt, wearing
    a bright yellow, Danskin tanktop
        (a glimpse of stocking?) & short blond hair—
    he tripped
    in an awkwardness not usually associated
    with homosexuals, turned
    to look at the pavement where it nudged him
        as if somehow the fault were there
    and not in his high shoes,
    his kinesthetic system.

I wanted
to reach to his shoulder & right him,
but he was too far away.

Such a mix of energies in this strange town,
this emerald city,
    like a microcosm
in which nothing
is looked on as something shocking:
greed grows
in the hearts of enough of us
to allay judgment; maybe the wrong way into it,
but the effect's the same—

a dozen or so
obvious pupils from the local school
stand in a cluster
against the deli window
    punching and touching each other
quietly baiting
the unmixed couples who pass them;
they don't know yet
what side
their bread's buttered on—

and the women and men we might have become
(a little hip, knowledgeable, and vague)
    glance shy and sidelong
over their glasses, in a kind
of indiscriminate longing,
    at the half-dressed
counter-jet-set children
milling in the street in front of the bakery
and the gay walkers.

Righting himself
the young man looked the other way as he passed me,
    obviously embarrassed and flustered,
having revealed, what? that he was awkward? yes,

and vulnerable—
then worked
to resume quickly enough
the grace of his passive
stalking.

Does it sound strange
when I call you beloved? well
    what else but a little honesty to save us:
we see, daily, the ones lacking luster
wanting to touch women who will return love,
failing—
      and then, desperate—
wanting anyone who will warm them,
the turning of any key.

And I'm desirous of something
I can't put my finger on this morning,
    but there's a slight urgency
as if the water were rising
and my finger itched for the dike.

It is raining a bit,
and I suspect this early
the streets of Provincetown are half slick,
half empty—
        it's something about history
I'm desiring: my own doings last night
and ours left
only half done
in the more distant past.

After the young man and I
had done our little dance together,

I went to see *Islands in the Stream*
that Hemingway story;

you know what they say about Old Hem,
his macho sense
and his use of the word "clean"—
it's those
psychological closet critics
    somehow fearing his sentence power
wanting to denude his art
by hitting his gone life—
        I don't mean to get literary.

In *Islands*
it was the play of history that got me:
    the three sons, by the two wives,
grown into the characteristics of their mothers,
and the artist father
who loved and regretted them
at the same time
    (some typical Hemingway fish battles)
till the oldest one died
trying to be like he thought his father was,
and then the father dying
in battle, fulfilling
the son's skewed vision of his power.

What was missing was the prose of course:
that needful tension of control
    in a world where anything goes
and could come apart—
but it wasn't a bad movie.

I got out and went to the bakery,
picked out a few sweets,

and headed for the pier to eat them
before going home.

It was very dark there,
noise and sights
of the emerald city behind me,
    some quiet lovers strolling,
and the jeweled lights of a few boats bobbing
at their moorings—

then I had this childish daydream:

The three of us are sitting in that room together
in California, 16 years ago—you
    and I, and that
thin young man
in his seduction garments. It gets late,
the Brubeck tape runs out
(he's a kind of anonymous servant) and when
    we send him to turn the reel over
he trips a little, becoming
suddenly
more than just visible,
and we laugh with him.

Beloved,
there's a power that steers these boats
I see on the bay, in the daytime
turning, often with graceless moves
    as if held in some anonymous matrix:
it's fish of course,
but that's only by implication,
        until they are pulled
streaming with seaweed and water
onto the decks, flooded with their presence—

And the town is
much more than the town's heritage,
is the young men walking
the town's streets even in a gentle rain,
    and the discovery only
about 5 years ago, that I might have turned that way
but didn't: I can see it all
as if through a dike or a keyhole
into the really conventional presence
of another place.

I don't mean
cheek against cheek or a drag dance, unhappy
gigolos, or vaseline, or some
    semi-professional groping
along some boardwalk,
under which fish in the dark feed
on the crumbs from hot dog rolls and hot nuts—
you put
your hand on my shoulder, one of the few times
we touched each other. It was never
in games, rituals, or fancy clothes
    that we passed those years together

but (tho sacrosanct) in the warm and abiding
ways of our own flesh,
Morris.

Standard-12,
You Stepped Out of a Dream (of Power)

I dreamt I saw your mother teaching a class
in which we all sat
    a little squeezed down in our seats.
She wore a hat
and under the brim her eyes burned
in and out,
her skull impossibly aflame
       under that power-mantle;
and our faces flushed because we were ashamed,
who could not answer a single question
that she'd asked.

    And in the middle row
a woman had wet her pants, her head
hid in her arms;
       the urine flowing from her cunt
had puddled on the floor and seemed
the only sweetness in the room—
and we were drawn to her.

Although she was a spy,
she'd held the answers back,
    had changed her loyalty in our midst,
and in her effort wet herself
and I could taste
some curative
in her urine on the deck.

    The classroom was a ship—
Your mother
cracked her ruler on the wheel,
her breath went in

and came out
acid accusation on the wind
and etched our faces
with these lines
of age and ignorance.

It was a sea dream—
and the ship meandered
and the uncontrolled woman took the helm
    and forced the cutter to its course

    and forced your mother
into staggering
underneath her crown, her power
now enfeebled,
    and our laughter
now that we were cared for
ringing in her ears—
        who reeled against the railing
as the ship came in
and fled along the gangway
to the dock.

Her power-mantle lay
in the puddle of urine on the deck,
and as the ship took sail again
    our new teacher picked it up
and put it
like a tilted sailor's cap upon her head
and told us of another dream,
another sea tale
& awakening—

She
who from her endomorphic rage

woke up again, in the little lights
of altar candles
    and the cinnamon body oil,
and he who only dimly
thought that he had wakened her
        (could therefore
    place a cherry in her navel
and worry it with his tongue
in that slow way of his
while he was eating it)
could steer her into matrices
her husband had refused her;
    only the little body's exit
from her womb
as she had splayed herself
had given her
such power.

    And that he called her
"Goddess at whose feet I kneel"
annealed her
and she took him masterfully
into her own life, on her own terms.

And she was larger than he was
and huge to him,
    in translation of his mother's power
that lingered over him
        but in her flesh
became the mother he had always wanted.

    Wives are like our mothers [Fantan says].
    When we were small our mothers fed us.
    When we are grown our wives cook for us.

If there is something good,
they keep it in the pot until we come home.

When we were small we slept with our mothers;
when we are grown we sleep with our wives.
Sometimes
when we are grown
    we wake in the night
    and call our wives
    mother—

There you have
    pathology of the dream
the teacher said, its politics—

But the woman lay
enchanted in her power, that place
where mothers die,
and the childish father that he was to her
    went up in incense smoke—
her tongue between his toes,
the forceful sucking of his sex.

And that he rightly felt
there is no root but this,
    no power and care.
He sucked her nipples for their juice;
they saw things in a clearer light
and eye to eye.

I woke
and thought of Kathy and the Old Manse,
    the way the woman had used
her diamond ring to carve
the message in the window glass:

futility of name and date,
her wedding night.

I'd made a joke
    that didn't seem too funny when I woke,
that underneath the futile tracings
were the real words:
sex is life.

There was no other lesson
for me to take, except
I spend time at the sea
and if
within some sickness
    you became incontinent
I'd wipe your urine up
and I would suck the rag.

But the ship of love,
now powered by body's energy
    of such learning
in the coda of the dream
set out through fog (recessional)
to search
increasing clarity at sea.

And the Catholic, white
and summer knicker uniforms that we wore
    gave way to open classroom
as your mother's ruler
changed to a jeweled scepter on the desk
and was no longer a fearful weapon
but an instrument of charts—
        the newly hardening needle
of a human compass

that our new teacher
placed with reverence on the map.

The cutter banked
to a certain course against the sea,
    and as the ship came
momentarily broadside to the distant dock
we peered intently
from our childish comfort
at the windy rail,

and saw
the tortured, desperate woman
wave her hanky at us from the quay,
and we were waving also
as the ship turned
and she shrunk away,

and then we heard the ringing
of the school's little bells,
the peal, and falling of the leaves,

and we sang—

Goodbye, Mother.
Goodbye,

speck.

Standard–14, Bye Bye Blackbird (Toby Olshin)

Somehow,
    beautiful small bird
this morning, at the window; one
always seems to come
when he is needed: this one,
        a slice of crescent rust,
white belly and delicate
thin beak
    (nameless, without field guide)
though smaller than a towhee
he resembles, stays
only a moment (here
in the country) to give a start to this.

But first, of care and woe, the nameless
to pack it up
    in weak and sufficient
simile: a towhee
winging slowly among branches
    in the night, like a fan, those
cuts of rust—
seen, and not seen
completely, but identified;
always, it is harder
with females.

Sweet sugar of the night, night
trails in the air:
    birds the color of night,
black birds, and the creak
of gray mourning doves
sweeter than sugar.

Night's
a prologue to day, though alive:
drunks, in rage on the city's streets,
inarticulate voices
        came to me; I fancied
lost day-birds calling, an air
and an airing, through spring's open windows,
thawed, lost, and winging low,
to give a start to this—
in a city

        where I was handed
hard luck stories in shrillness,
sugar or caffeine,
the fix of your fame in public,
our name still a confusion:
        I got your letters, perverted
messages in a box. Heads
turned still when I spoke our name.

What can I give you?
permutations of Duv, Tobe and Ocean?
        Peace, of our country name?
I'll hold it for you now,
light the light, in secret?

I'll take our name
into the night, not of towhee
in shyness, but beat of the name's
echo in the mouth, "Toby"—
        to soothe even these dark birds
in the chest, trail them
from force of anxiety of lost name—
here, in the country.

But it is morning. It is not night
nor country. It's the becalmed
          waters of ocean at bayside,
the sharp glint of white sails in the sunrise,
green sea lettuce at shoreline, that
small bird at the feeder—
(forgiving light)
          and a need
for celebration beyond the name's hoard,
where he waits for me:
a confusing spring warbler (or is it a she?
cuts of rust?)
     this music the day makes
that we could dance to. You
          and I walk on the beach together;
we are thankful for no language:
yellow hulls in the sunrise, terns in the air...
Surely, there is some better message
I can send you?

I'm blue again, love struck
for the dead; words stick
     like a shocked wisdom tooth,
useless in the mouth
and out of it: just another
dumb simile; is the life
but a metaphor? Death is the ground
of the memory
     which *is* the life, not spirit
but that which the hand opens to: (the memory)
tracings in palm lines,
rust cuts, that become "Toby" or any name;
only, that the brand burns in—

and that I can think of cowboys (here
at the sea?)
    and a hat you once wore.
I caught a glimpse of
you, cowgirl on the avenue,
corner of Broad & Arch (in a city)
      who didn't see me, was intent
as always, on the task at hand—
in this case hitchhiking
in a transit strike.

Your hat sat
at rakish angle, but for others; un-
selfconscious in any costume
alert, always ready (for what?) for
anything: memos, empty hassles, dancing,
I think, even
    that final activity, the loose end
of which I am left with: "Toby"
on scraps of paper
    awkward voices on a phone,
the push of memories that can't be filed
or put away with you; it calls back to me
constantly—
    Duv, Tobe, and Ocean
belongs in the country
but *I'm* near the changing patterns
at shoreline, and there is no
peace, here, yet.

        (Peace—
permutations of the name come to that:
English, into Hebrew, into English:
Toby—as peacefulness.)

I picked you up, your smile was
wan, already. One

note, one
song stroke, one throat, one
bird, only, to evoke the name,
the insane desire for a perfect speech:
(blackbird) here I go—

Let me forget, darling, that I go on
living; let the name be
      not a mask, but a forgiving
presence; let our face turn
waxen, then insubstantial; let
features be rust cuts on this evoking body.

To dance, to
hum to the tune while dancing, to discover,
dear memory, in this way, the late arrival,
the bed made, and the light lit.

There was light's flicker at shoreline: night
lights on the draggers; at night
      light of phosphorus; she was white, in the moon's light
or candle flame, the light she had lit.
In day's light
sun forced upon her that blindness,
her face screwed up squinting
      in the cruelest of lights
which reflects back:
a bright skull.
            That was in a city
of variety and careful distance
and guarding,
where she carried her name in a manner

479

of fame, an aggressive
presence (he felt bereft of it).

But this was at the very edge of the sea;
it was night;
    there were fishermen in mackinaws, hats
reminiscent of cowboys,
poles, stuck in the sand, and standing;
it was cold (clouds covered the moon now).

And she went out from the light
in neuter garments;
    it was dark, she was passing,
and they called out to her—ignorant
and stupid—not seeing
she was a woman (their expectations):
    she had a rigged pole
and a gear box; she was passing
beyond their intelligence.
Really,
she was engaged in a kind of dancing:
steps, secret and special, that were acceptable,
because they were too subtle
for them. She passed along and behind them,
came to a place at line's end,
    at the headland, faced out
to becalmed ocean, and then she really passed.

He, then, at the promontory
in that masculine line:
no women, cold weather, and the place
lacked flavor.
    It was very much like dancing
(in ego) without a partner; blues
and striped bass passing, beyond the bait.

It was dark, there were no birds
visible, no calls.
    He thought of the made bed
behind him, the light lit,
and he pushed the crown of his hat down,
gathered the gear up, and headed back.

Toby,
the sun rises into the clouds
and the wind comes in
    (a strange morning)—
it is clearer, as the light softens;
the clouds are high
and cirrus, but they contain
rain: drops already
    on the pine's new candles, some
bent in the wind.
To sing (of memory, rust) is harder now,
the day so real and the night spent.
In what way can I leave you?

There are birds waiting, or preening
or exchanging places in the limbs,
in the rain:
    the receding brown of females,
feathers lifted in the wind,
        rust cuts on the males.
No (rust is in memory), these cuts
are arterial red.
Somehow,
    sun breaks through in places;
the blackbirds turn into it,
and their breasts swell.

Acknowledgements

The poems collected here previously appeared in the following volumes:

Maps, Perishable Press, Mount Horeb, WI, 1969
Worms into Nails, Perishable Press, Mount Horeb, WI, 1969
The Brand, Perishable Press, Mount Horeb, WI, 1969
The Hawk-Foot Poems, Abraxas Press, Madison, WI, 1969
Pig/s Book, Doctor Generosity Press, New York, 1969
Vectors, Albatross Press & Ziggurat / Membrane Press, Milwaukee, WI, 1972
Fishing, Perishable Press, Mt Horeb, WI, 1974
City, Membrane Press, Milwaukee, WI, 1974
The Wrestlers, and other poems, Barlenmir House, New York, 1974
Changing Appearance, Membrane Press, Milwaukee, WI, 1975
Home, Membrane Press, Milwaukee, WI, 1976
Doctor Miriam, Perishable Press, Mt Horeb, WI, 1977
Aesthetics, Membrane Press, Milwaukee, WI, 1978
The Florence Poems, Permanent Press, London & New York, 1978
Still / Quiet, Landlocked Press, Madison, WI, 1979
Birdsongs, Perishable Press. Mt Horeb, WI, 1980
Two Standards, Salient Seedling Press, Madison, WI, 1982
Sitting in Gusevik, Madison, WI, 1983
We Are the Fire, New Directions, New York, 1984

Four poems from *Home* and *Bird Songs* were set to music by
the composer Paul Epstein, and performed in Philadelphia.

Poems in this volume have appeared, in roughly chronological order
in the following magazines:

*Caterpillar, Choice, Confrontation, First Issue, For Now, From a Window, Gnosis,
Helicon, Hika, Inside Outer Space, Intrepid, Loam, Maps, The Minnesota Review,
Mulch, The Nation, The New York Quarterly, The Poetry Bag, Sumac, Trace,
Transition, Vincent, Win, Works, Abraxas, The American Experience, Athanor,
Broadway Boogie, Desperado, Equal Time, The Falcon, 42nd Street Trip, The
Friendly Local Press, Gegenschein Quarterly, Goat's Head, Helicon, Lillabulero,
Loam, Loose Change, Spark, Damascus Road, Letters, Loves etc, New Directions
#25, Occurrence, Stations, The Chicago Review, Works, Handbook, Sixpack, The
American Poetry Review, The Mysterious Barricades, The Valley Advocate, Anima,
Cottonwood Review, Longhouse, Tracks, Sun and Moon, Montemora, Boundary 2,
Conjunctions, Delirium, The John O'Hara Review, Poetry Now, Tamarisk, Tracks,
Albatross, Lion Head, The Painted Bride Quarterly, Paper Air,* and *Tractor.*

Milton Keynes UK
Ingram Content Group UK Ltd.
UKHW041906231223
434901UK00003B/48

9 781848 6192